YOUR recipe could appear in our next cookbook!

Share your tried & true family favorites with us instantly at

www.gooseberrypatch.com

If you'd rather jot 'em down by hand, just mail this form to...

Gooseberry Patch • Cookbooks – Call for Recipes
PO Box 812 • Columbus, OH 43216-0812

If your recipe is selected for a book, you'll receive a FREE copy!

Please share only your original recipes or those that you have made your own over the years.

Recipe Name:

Number of Servings:

Any fond memories about this recipe? Special touches you like to add or handy shortcuts?

Ingredients (include specific measurements):

Instructions (continue on back if needed):

Special Code: **cookbookspage**

Over ↗

Extra space for recipe if needed:

Tell us about yourself...

Your complete contact information is needed so that we can send you your FREE cookbook, if your recipe is published. Phone numbers and email addresses are kept private and will only be used if we have questions about your recipe.

Name:

Address:

City: State: Zip:

Email:

Daytime Phone:

Thank you! Vickie & Jo Ann

Fresh
Farmhouse
Recipes

**Farm-fresh delicious dishes
made with wholesome ingredients**

Gooseberry Patch

An imprint of Globe Pequot
246 Goose Lane
Guilford, CT 06437

www.gooseberrypatch.com

1•800•854•6673

Do you have a tried & true recipe...

tip, craft or memory that you'd like to see featured in
a **Gooseberry Patch** cookbook? Visit our website at
www.gooseberrypatch.com and follow the
easy steps to submit your favorite family recipe.
Or send them to us at:

Gooseberry Patch
PO Box 812
Columbus, OH 43216-0812

Don't forget to include the number of servings your recipe makes,
plus your name, address, phone number and email address. If we
select your recipe, your name will appear right along with it...
and you'll receive a **FREE** copy of the book!

Contents

Dedication

To everyone who loves the first farmstand of the season and the first bite of a juicy sun-ripened tomato or a buttery ear of sweet corn.

Appreciation

A big thanks to each of our friends for sharing your best, most fresh and flavorful recipes.

Breakfast Sunny-Side Up

FRESH FARMHOUSE
Recipes

Dutch Apple Oven Pancake

Linda Belon
Wintersville, OH

*This is delicious and so simple...easier than making
separate pancakes to serve four. We love it!*

3 T. butter
2 apples, peeled, cored and sliced
1/2 t. cinnamon
2 eggs, beaten
1/2 c. milk

1/2 c. all-purpose flour
1/4 t. salt
1 t. vanilla extract
Garnish: powdered sugar

In an oven-safe 10" skillet, melt butter over medium heat. Add apples
and cook until tender. Stir in cinnamon; set aside. In a large bowl,
combine eggs, milk, flour and salt. Beat with an electric mixer on
medium speed until smooth. Stir in vanilla. Pour batter over apples in
skillet. Place skillet on lowest oven rack and bake at 450 degrees for
10 minutes. Reduce oven to 350 degrees. Bake 5 to 10 minutes more,
until pancake is puffy and golden. Sprinkle generously with powdered
sugar. Cut into wedges and serve warm. Serves 4.

Wake up to colorful pottery on the breakfast table...so cheery.
Search tag sales for whimsical hens on nests or
cream pitcher cows. What treasures!

6

Breakfast Sunny-Side Up

Garden-Fresh Tomato Pie

Gladys Kielar
Whitehouse, OH

I have served this for breakfast, lunch and dinner...
it's welcome anytime!

9-inch pie crust, unbaked
1 c. shredded Monterey
   Jack cheese
2 ripe tomatoes, cut into wedges
1 t. dried oregano

1 t. dried basil
1/8 t. pepper
2 green onions, thinly sliced
2 T. soft bread crumbs
2 T. butter, melted

Crimp edges of pie crust; pierce bottom of crust several times with a fork. Bake at 425 degrees for 15 minutes, or until lightly golden; let cool. Sprinkle cheese into crust. Arrange tomato wedges in a circular pattern around the edge of pie crust. Sprinkle seasonings over tomatoes. Sprinkle onions in the center. Sprinkle with bread crumbs; drizzle with melted butter. Bake at 425 degrees for 20 minutes, or until golden. Allow to cool for at least 10 minutes; cut into wedges. Makes 6 servings.

Make a quick, savory crumb crust for a quiche. Spread 2-1/2 tablespoons softened butter in a pie plate, then firmly press 2-1/2 cups crisp cracker crumbs into the butter. Freeze until firm, spoon in filling and bake as directed.

FRESH FARMHOUSE
Recipes

Pear-Zucchini Muffins

Christy Doughty
Dexter, OR

I always get raves for these muffins! If you don't have any wheat germ on hand, omit it and increase the whole-wheat flour to one cup.

4 ripe pears, cored and chopped
1 c. zucchini, shredded
1 c. sugar
1 c. brown sugar, packed
3 eggs, beaten
1 c. oil
1 T. vanilla extract
3/4 c. chopped walnuts or pecans

2 c. all-purpose flour
1/2 c. whole-wheat flour
1/2 c. wheat germ
1/2 t. baking powder
1 t. baking soda
1/2 t. salt
2 t. pumpkin pie spice

In a large bowl, combine pears, zucchini, sugars, eggs, oil, vanilla and nuts. Mix well and set aside. In another bowl, combine remaining ingredients; stir into pear mixture until well blended. Spoon batter into 30 paper-lined muffin cups, filling 3/4 full. Bake at 350 degrees for 22 to 26 minutes. Makes 2-1/2 dozen.

Pair a basket of warm muffins with a crock of fruit butter...yum! Simply blend 1/2 cup each of softened butter and strawberry, apricot or peach preserves.

Breakfast Sunny-Side Up

Farmhouse Scrambled Eggs

Diana Chaney
Olathe, KS

*Extra good made with farm-fresh eggs...a delicious way
to use up all those odds & ends of veggies!*

4 t. olive oil
1 small zucchini, diced
1 ripe tomato, diced
8 eggs

2 T. milk
salt and pepper to taste
1 c. fresh baby spinach, packed
1/4 c. shredded Parmesan cheese

Heat olive oil in a skillet over medium heat. Add zucchini; cook and stir just until tender, about one minute. Stir in tomato; reduce heat to medium-low. Meanwhile, beat eggs in a large bowl. Whisk in milk, salt and pepper until frothy; add to skillet. Cook, stirring occasionally, until partially set. Add spinach and cheese; stir gently. Cook for one more minute, or until eggs are completely set and still moist. Serves 4.

Honey Peach Smoothie

Marla Kinnersley
Highlands Ranch, CO

*This is such a refreshing smoothie when peaches are in season.
We leave the skin on the peaches and it tastes amazing. Can't get
enough of this at our house!*

1 ripe peach, quartered and pitted
1 c. plain yogurt
1/2 t. vanilla extract

1 t. honey
1 c. ice cubes

Combine all ingredients in a blender; process until smooth. Divide between 2 glasses; add straws and serve. Makes 2 servings.

For the fluffiest scrambled eggs ever,
try a farmhouse secret...stir in
a pinch of baking powder.

FRESH FARMHOUSE
Recipes

Cherry Crumb Coffee Cake

Vickie Wiseman
Liberty Twp., OH

This is a recipe that Mom made quite often, since one of the houses where we lived had a cherry tree. This recipe is so much better with fresh cherries, but canned cherries work well too.

1/4 c. shortening
3/4 c. sugar
1 egg, beaten
1/2 c. milk or light cream

1-1/2 c. all-purpose flour
2 t. baking powder
1/2 t. salt
1 lb. sour pie cherries, pitted

In a large bowl, blend together shortening and sugar. Beat in egg. Blend in milk or cream; set aside. In another bowl, mix together flour, baking powder and salt; add to shortening mixture and mix well. Spread batter in a greased 9"x9" baking pan. Arrange cherries over batter. Sprinkle with Crumb Topping. Bake at 375 degrees for 30 to 35 minutes. Makes 10 to 12 servings.

Crumb Topping:

1/2 c. all-purpose flour
1/2 c. brown sugar, packed

1/4 t. cinnamon
1/4 c. butter, melted

Mix together flour, brown sugar and cinnamon. Add melted butter and blend well.

Enjoy favorite breakfast foods with your family at dinnertime! A simple omelet or frittata is perfect. Just add a basket of muffins, fresh fruit and a steamy pot of tea.

Breakfast Sunny-Side Up

Spinach & Mushroom Quiche

Judy Lange
Imperial, PA

So yummy! This is a Christmas favorite at our house, but too good to make just once a year. If you'd like to use fresh mushrooms, sauté them in a little butter before adding to the crust.

10-oz. pkg. fresh spinach
9-inch frozen pie crust, unbaked
1/4 to 1/2 c. real bacon bits
4-oz. can sliced mushrooms, drained

8 eggs
2/3 c. milk
8-oz. pkg. shredded Cheddar cheese

Spread spinach evenly in unbaked pie crust. Top with bacon bits and mushrooms; set aside. Beat eggs in a large bowl; whisk in milk. Pour into crust; top evenly with cheese. Bake at 350 degrees for 50 minutes. Let stand several minutes; cut into wedges. Serves 6 to 8.

Fresh mushrooms are flavorful, filling and low in calories. Add them to egg dishes, soups and wherever else you'd like a punch of flavor. Store mushrooms, unwashed, in a paper bag in the fridge.

FRESH FARMHOUSE
Recipes

Apple-Pecan Baked Oatmeal
Marcia Marcoux
Charlton, MA

I have made this so many times when I have guests for breakfast or brunch...it's always a crowd-pleaser!

5 Granny Smith apples, peeled, cored and chopped
1/2 c. chopped pecans, toasted
18-oz. pkg. old-fashioned oats, uncooked
3 eggs, beaten
1 c. brown sugar, packed
1 c. unsweetened applesauce

1 T. cinnamon
4 t. baking powder
1 t. salt
1 t. vanilla extract
1-1/4 c. water
1 c. milk
1/4 c. butter, melted
Garnish: warm maple syrup

Spread apples in a lightly greased 13"x9" glass baking pan; sprinkle with pecans. In a large bowl, combine remaining ingredients except garnish; stir until well blended. Spoon evenly over apple mixture. Cover and bake at 350 degrees for 30 minutes. Uncover and bake 20 minutes more, or until set and golden. Do not overbake. Serve with warm maple syrup. Serves 8 to 10.

Try steel-cut oats in recipes that call for regular long-cooking oats. Steel-cut oats are less processed, for a pleasing chewy texture you're sure to enjoy.

Summer Hash

Jess Brunink
Whitehall, MI

A great meatless hash for summertime, when all your veggies are ripe and ready to enjoy. This is really hearty for breakfast, and also makes a great side dish with dinner.

1 lb. redskin potatoes, halved
1 T. olive oil
1 green pepper, diced
3/4 c. onion, diced
1 yellow squash, diced

6 to 8 okra pods, sliced
   1/2-inch thick
1 t. garlic, minced
salt to taste
Optional: favorite salsa

In a saucepan, cover potatoes with water. Bring to a boil over high heat and cook until fork-tender. Drain; dice cooled potatoes. Add oil to a skillet. Add potatoes and remaining ingredients except optional salsa to pan. Cook over medium-high heat for 10 minutes; stir. Cover and cook over medium heat for 30 minutes more, stirring every few minutes. If desired, serve topped with salsa. Serves 8.

I have never had so many good ideas day after day
as when I worked in the garden.
—John Erskine

FRESH FARMHOUSE
Recipes

Sweet Onion Omelet

Vickie
Gooseberry Patch

This is the tastiest omelet you'll ever have!

1 sweet onion, chopped
1 T. butter
3 eggs, beaten
3 T. milk

salt and pepper to taste
1 ripe tomato, sliced
1/4 to 1/2 c. shredded Cheddar
   cheese

In a skillet over medium heat, sauté onion in butter until translucent; set aside. In a bowl, lightly whisk together eggs, milk, salt and pepper; add to onion mixture in skillet. Cook until eggs are set on the bottom. Gently lift sides with a spatula to allow uncooked portion to run underneath; cook until nearly set. Arrange tomato slices on half of the omelet. Top with cheese; fold in half and turn onto a serving plate. Makes 2 to 3 servings.

Asparagus, Bacon & Eggs

Wendy Ball
Battle Creek, MI

The first time I made this, I used soft-boiled eggs, spooned over steamed asparagus. This is a variation of that...who doesn't like a little bacon with their eggs?

1/2 to 1 lb. bacon, cut into
   1-inch pieces
1 lb. fresh asparagus, cut into
   1-inch pieces

4 eggs, soft-boiled, poached or
   scrambled (see page 36)
salt and pepper to taste

In a skillet over medium heat, cook bacon to desired crispness; drain. Add asparagus and stir-fry until tender-crisp. Meanwhile, prepare eggs as desired. Divide bacon mixture among 4 plates or bowls. Top each portion with an egg. Makes 4 servings.

Honey comes in lots of flavor varieties. Seek out a local beekeeper at the farmers' market and try a few samples... you may find a new favorite!

Breakfast Sunny-Side Up

Poppy Seed Fruit Salad

Jo Ann
Gooseberry Patch

Mix it up! Orange sections, raspberries, kiwi fruit and honeydew cubes are delicious in this colorful salad too.

1/4 c. honey
1/4 c. frozen limeade
   concentrate, thawed
2 t. poppy seed
1 c. strawberries, hulled and
   halved

1 c. blueberries
1 c. pineapple cubes
1 c. watermelon cubes
1/4 c. slivered almonds, toasted
   if desired

Combine honey, limeade concentrate and poppy seed in a large bowl. Add fruit; toss gently to mix. Sprinkle with almonds. Serve immediately, or cover and chill. Makes 8 servings.

Treat yourself to an old farmhouse tradition...a big slice of apple or cherry pie for breakfast!

FRESH FARMHOUSE
Recipes

Zucchini Breakfast Casserole
Penny Sherman
Ava, MO

*On Saturday mornings, this dish really gets our family going before
we head out to the farmers' market, sports park or other fun together.
Crisp bacon and fruit muffins round out our meal.*

6 to 8 eggs
1 c. ricotta cheese
1 c. shredded Parmesan cheese
1/4 t. hot pepper sauce
1 t. salt
1/4 t. pepper

1-1/2 c. roma tomatoes, chopped
3 c. zucchini, grated
1/2 c. fresh basil, sliced
4 slices day-old country-style
    bread, cubed

Beat eggs in a large bowl. Add ricotta cheese; beat until smooth. Add
Parmesan cheese, hot sauce, salt and pepper; stir well and set aside.
Place tomatoes in a sieve; gently press out moisture and add tomatoes
to egg mixture. Repeat with zucchini; add to eggs along with basil.
Moisten bread cubes with a little water; squeeze out any excess moisture
using paper towels. Fold bread cubes into egg mixture. Spoon mixture
into a greased 13"x9" baking pan; even it out with spoon. Set pan on
center oven rack. Bake, uncovered, at 350 degrees for 30 minutes,
or until puffed and lightly golden. If a darker golden color is desired,
increase oven to 425 degrees; bake for another 5 to 10 minutes. Set
pan on a wire rack to cool for 10 minutes. Cut into squares to serve.
Serves 6 to 8.

To keep a chunk of fresh Parmesan cheese fresh longer,
wrap it in a paper towel that has been moistened with cider
vinegar, tuck into a plastic zipping bag and refrigerate.

Raspberry Muffins

Kim Ahmu
Independence, MO

These muffins are a favorite in our family, whether it's for breakfast, lunch or an after-dinner snack. This is a simple recipe that will allow you to use whatever soft fruit you have on hand. Strawberries are really good too!

1 egg, beaten	2 t. baking powder
1/2 c. milk	1/2 t. salt
1/4 c. oil	1/2 t. cinnamon
1-1/2 c. all-purpose flour	1 c. raspberries, thawed and
1/2 c. sugar	drained if frozen

In a large bowl, whisk together egg, milk and oil until well blended; set aside. In another bowl, stir together flour, sugar, baking powder, salt and cinnamon. Add flour mixture to egg mixture. Stir just until moistened; batter should be lumpy. Fold in raspberries. Spoon batter into 12 greased muffin cups, filling 2/3 full. Bake at 400 degrees for 20 to 25 minutes. Makes one dozen.

A baker's secret! Grease muffin cups on the bottoms
and just halfway up the sides. Muffins will bake up
nicely puffed on top.

FRESH FARMHOUSE
Recipes

Nutty Olive Oil Granola

Marcia Marcoux
Charlton, MA

*This tasty recipe has been shared with many friends and relatives.
Serve it topped with Greek yogurt and fruit, or simply munch on it
as is. It's great to keep on hand for guests!*

3 c. old-fashioned oats,
   uncooked
1-1/2 c. sliced almonds
1 c. chopped pecans
1 c. sweetened dried cranberries
   or raisins

3/4 c. pure maple syrup
1/2 c. brown sugar, packed
1/3 c. olive oil
1 t. kosher salt
1/2 t. cinnamon

In a large bowl, combine oats, nuts and cranberries; stir until well
mixed. In a small bowl, whisk together remaining ingredients. Pour over
oatmeal mixture and stir until well coated. Spray a large rimmed baking
sheet generously with non-stick vegetable spray. Spread mixture evenly
on pan in a single layer. Bake at 300 degrees for 45 minutes, stirring
every 15 minutes, or until golden and well toasted. Cool completely.
Store in an airtight container. Makes about 8 cups.

A warm fruit compote is delightful with breakfast. Simmer sliced
peaches, blueberries and raspberries together with a little honey,
lemon juice and cinnamon, just until syrupy and tender.
Scrumptious made with fresh ripe fruit!

Breakfast Sunny-Side Up

Feel-Good Berry Smoothie

Lori Williams
Acton, ME

This is a great breakfast or post-workout smoothie. For a tropical twist, I sometimes add pineapple juice or coconut extract, or both! This smoothie helps keep me healthy and fit during the tough Maine winters. A tasty guilt-free snack on hot summer days too!

1 c. fresh strawberries, hulled
   and halved
3/4 c. fresh raspberries or
   blackberries
1 c. fat-free plain Greek yogurt

1 c. frozen blueberries
1 c. 5-calorie cranberry juice
   drink
1 T. chia seed or flax seed

Add ingredients to a blender in the order listed. Pulse until mixture comes together. Process on high speed for about one minute, until smooth, adding a little more juice, if needed. Pour into one large glass or 2 smaller glasses. Serves one to 2.

Honeydew Breakfast Bowls

Cheri Maxwell
Gulf Breeze, FL

Yum! This is delicious with a juicy ripe cantaloupe melon too. Use your favorite berries, or mix 'em up.

16-oz. container plain
   Greek yogurt
1 honeydew melon, halved
   and seeded

1/2 c. berries, thawed if frozen
1/2 c. favorite granola
Optional: honey to taste

Divide yogurt between melon halves. Top with berries and granola; drizzle with honey, if desired. Serves 2.

A nutritious breakfast in a hurry! Toast half a whole-grain bagel, then top with reduced-fat cream cheese and sliced fresh strawberries.

FRESH FARMHOUSE
Recipes

Overnight Berry French Toast

Nancy Wise
Little Rock, AR

*This recipe is really scrumptious! It's simple to make...I made
two pans to serve to guests at my daughter's wedding brunch.
Mix & match the most luscious fresh berries you can find!*

1-lb. loaf country-style bread,
   cut into 1-inch cubes
8 eggs, beaten
2-1/2 c. milk
1/2 c. sugar
1/2 c. brown sugar, packed
1 T. vanilla extract
1 t. cinnamon

1 t. ground ginger
1/2 t. nutmeg
1/4 t. salt
3 c. fresh strawberries,
   blueberries and/or raspberries
sugar to taste
Garnish: powdered sugar
Optional: maple syrup

Spread bread cubes evenly in a buttered 13"x9" baking pan; set aside. In
a large bowl, whisk together eggs, milk, sugars, vanilla, spices and salt.
Carefully pour over bread. Cover with plastic wrap and refrigerate
overnight. In the morning, uncover; bake at 350 degrees for 45 to
60 minutes, to desired texture. Toss berries with sugar as desired. Top
servings with berries, powdered sugar and maple syrup, if desired.
Serves 8 to 10.

Waffles with whipped cream and fruit...is there a more delicious
way to begin the day? Spread ripe blueberries in a single layer on
a baking sheet and freeze until solid, then store them in plastic
freezer bags. Then you'll be able to enjoy them year 'round!

Breakfast
Sunny-Side Up

Spring Rhubarb Muffins

Janis Parr
Ontario, Canada

Use fresh rhubarb from the garden or farmers' market for these delicious muffins. They are moist and flavorful...freeze well, too!

1-1/4 c. all-purpose flour
1-1/2 t. baking powder
1 t. salt
1/2 t. cinnamon
1/4 c. sugar
1/4 c. brown sugar, packed

1 egg, beaten
1/2 c. milk
1/4 c. oil
1/4 t. almond extract
1-1/2 c. fresh rhubarb, diced
Optional: additional sugar

In a large bowl, combine flour, baking powder, salt, cinnamon and sugars; mix well and set aside. In a smaller bowl, whisk together egg, milk, oil and extract. Pour egg mixture over flour mixture; stir just until moistened. Fold in rhubarb. Spoon batter into 8 greased large muffin cups, filling 2/3 full. Bake at 375 degrees for 20 to 25 minutes, until a toothpick inserted in the center tests done. If desired, sprinkle muffins with additional sugar while still warm. Makes 8 large muffins.

Fresh rhubarb tends to absorb water easily, so clean stalks
with a dampened paper towel rather than rinsing
under running water.

FRESH FARMHOUSE
Recipes

Sarah's Zucchini Quiche

Sarah Gruber
Monroe, MI

Every summer, I turn to this recipe when the zucchini in my garden starts producing so abundantly. Browned Italian sausage, chopped ham or cooked, crumbled bacon may be substituted for the breakfast sausage. For a lighter quiche, leave out the sausage...it'll still be delicious! For a spicier bite, switch out the Cheddar cheese for Pepper Jack.

1 lb. ground pork breakfast
    sausage
4 eggs, lightly beaten
1/2 c. biscuit baking mix
1/4 t. salt
1/4 t. pepper
1/4 t. garlic powder
2 t. dried, minced onions

3 c. zucchini, shredded
hot pepper sauce or red pepper
    flakes to taste
1/2 c. shredded Cheddar cheese
1/4 c. melted butter or olive oil
Optional: additional shredded
    cheese

Brown sausage in a skillet over medium heat; drain and add to a large bowl. Add remaining ingredients except optional cheese; stir together until well mixed. Pour mixture into a lightly greased 9" quiche pan or 9"x9" baking pan. Bake at 375 degrees for 35 minutes, or until cooked through and golden on top. Remove from oven; sprinkle with additional cheese, if desired. Let stand for 5 minutes; cut into wedges or squares. Makes 8 servings.

For a casual brunch, serve breakfast favorites on cheery blue and white dishes arranged on homespun placemats. Tuck a bouquet of daisies or zinnias into a big Mason jar!

Breakfast Sunny-Side Up

Parmesan & Cheddar Grits

Amy Butcher
Columbus, GA

Being from Georgia, we love our grits! I serve them alongside scrambled eggs and bacon. Sometimes I'll serve this recipe at dinnertime, topped with shrimp and sweet red peppers sautéed in butter. Yum!

6 c. water
1-1/2 c. quick-cooking grits,
   uncooked
1 c. shredded sharp Cheddar
   cheese

1/2 c. shredded Parmesan
   cheese
2 T. half-and-half
1/2 t. salt
1/4 t. pepper

In a large saucepan, bring water to a boil. Slowly stir in grits. Reduce heat to medium-low; cover and cook until thickened, about 5 minutes, stirring occasionally. Remove from heat; stir in remaining ingredients. Cover to keep warm until serving time. Makes 6 servings.

Breakfast sliders! Whip up your favorite pancake batter and make silver dollar-size pancakes. Sandwich them together with slices of heat & serve sausage. Serve with maple syrup on the side for dipping...yum!

FRESH FARMHOUSE
Recipes

Cinnamon Oat Bread

Diane Omiotek
Burlington, ON

*This tasty bread is so simple to make...great for breakfast,
with a cup of hot tea. Sometimes I like to add 1/2 cup raisins
or chopped walnuts.*

1 c. quick-cooking oats,
   uncooked
1-1/2 c. boiling water
1/2 c. butter
1 c. sugar
1 c. brown sugar, packed

2 eggs
1 t. vanilla extract
1-3/4 c. all-purpose flour
1 t. baking soda
1/2 t. salt
1-1/8 t. cinnamon

Place oats in a small heat-proof bowl. Pour boiling water over oats and
set aside. In a large bowl, with an electric mixer on low speed, beat
butter until creamy. Gradually add sugars, beating until well blended.
Add eggs, one at a time, beating well after each addition. Beat in
vanilla; set aside. In another bowl, combine flour, baking soda, salt and
cinnamon; mix well. Gradually add flour mixture to butter mixture and
stir until smooth. Stir in oats mixture. Spoon batter into a greased and
floured 9"x5" loaf pan. Bake at 350 degrees for about one hour, until
a toothpick inserted in center of loaf comes out clean. Cool loaf in pan
for 10 minutes; turn out onto a wire rack to cool completely. Makes
one loaf.

A whistling teakettle adds cheer to any kitchen. It's easy to
remove the hard water and lime build-up in a yard-sale find. Just
pour in 2 cups of white vinegar and bring to a boil. Simmer for
10 minutes, then rinse well...ready to brew up a cup of tea.

Breakfast Sunny-Side Up

Yummy Peach Freezer Jam

Claudia Keller
Carrollton, GA

Summer in a jar! It isn't just for spreading on toast. Stir a spoonful into warm breakfast oatmeal...yum!

2 lbs. ripe peaches, peeled,
  pitted and finely chopped
4-1/2 c. sugar
2 T. lemon juice
3/4 c. water

1-3/4 oz. pkg. powdered fruit
  pectin
6 1/2-pint plastic freezer jars
  and lids, sterilized

Measure exactly 3 cups chopped peaches into a large bowl. Add sugar and lemon juice; mix well. Let stand for 10 minutes, stirring occasionally. Meanwhile, combine water and pectin in a small saucepan over high heat. Bring to a boil, stirring constantly. Cook and stir for one minute; add to peach mixture. Stir for 3 minutes, until sugar is dissolved. Ladle jam into jars, leaving 1/2-inch headspace. Wipe off top edges of containers; immediately cover with lids. Let stand at room temperature for 24 hours, to allow gel to set. Refrigerate up to 3 weeks or freeze up to one year. To use, thaw overnight in refrigerator. Makes 6, 1/2-pint jars.

Share your homemade goodies with a friend. Wrap fresh-baked muffins in a tea towel and tuck them into a basket along with a jar of jam. A sweet gift perfect for a new neighbor or a birthday girl!

FRESH FARMHOUSE
Recipes

Farmhouse Buckwheat Pancakes & Blueberry Syrup

Vickie
Gooseberry Patch

Our favorite weekend meal! On special occasions,
a dollop of whipped cream is a must.

1 c. buckwheat flour
1 c. all-purpose flour
2 T. sugar
4 t. baking powder
2 t. cinnamon

1/2 t. salt
2 c. whole milk
3 T. plus 2 t. canola oil, divided
2 eggs, beaten
Garnish: butter

In a large bowl, combine flours, sugar, baking powder, cinnamon and salt. Set aside. In another bowl, whisk together milk, 3 tablespoons oil and eggs. Add milk mixture to flour mixture, stirring until just blended. Spread remaining oil on a non-stick griddle pan or skillet; heat over medium heat until very hot. Drop batter onto pan by 1/3 cupfuls; cook until bubbles form on top. Flip pancakes and cook another minute, or until set. Serve with butter and Blueberry Syrup. Serves 4.

Blueberry Syrup:

1 pt. blueberries, thawed
   if frozen

1 c. sugar
1/4 c. water

Combine ingredients in a small saucepan and stir well. Cook over medium heat for 10 to 15 minutes, stirring until sugar dissolves and pressing berries against the side of pan, until syrupy and berries are softened. Serve warm or cool. Makes about 2-1/2 cups.

Making pancakes for a crowd? Stack them on a plate and slide into a 175-degree oven. They'll stay warm until serving time.

Breakfast Sunny-Side Up

Spicy Maple-Glazed Bacon

Tonya Sheppard
Galveston, TX

So, so good! The richness of the bacon and the sweetness of the maple syrup are enhanced by the warm spices. Great for breakfast...very popular at parties too!

1 lb. bacon
2 t. chili powder
1/4 t. cayenne pepper
1/4 t. curry powder
1/4 t. cinnamon
6 T. pure maple syrup, divided

Arrange bacon slices on a rack set in an ungreased 15"x10" jelly-roll pan. Combine spices; sprinkle half of mixture over bacon. Turn over bacon slices and sprinkle with remaining spice mixture. Bake at 450 degrees for 10 minutes. Drizzle or brush with 2 tablespoons syrup; turn bacon over and drizzle with remaining syrup. Bake for 6 to 10 minutes longer, until crisp and golden. Drain on paper towels; serve warm. Serves 8, 2 slices each.

A hearty farmstyle breakfast that's welcome on the chilliest morning! Cook up diced potatoes in a cast-iron skillet, then use the back of a spoon to make 6 wells. Break an egg into each and bake at 350 degrees for 12 to 14 minutes, until eggs are set. Serve piping hot, right from the skillet.

FRESH FARMHOUSE
Recipes

Garden-Style Breakfast Bowls   *Marlene Darnell*
Newport Beach, CA

*After breakfasting on these hearty bowls, we're set for a
busy day. Add a sprinkle of hot pepper sauce and some
shredded Cheddar cheese, if you like.*

4 eggs, poached (see page 36)
2 t. olive oil
2 c. sliced mushrooms
4 c. fresh spinach, chopped
15-1/2 oz. can cannellini beans,
    drained and rinsed

1 c. cherry tomatoes, quartered
salt and pepper to taste
Optional: 1/4 c. chopped green
    onions

Poach eggs as desired. Meanwhile, heat oil in a skillet over medium
heat. Add mushrooms and cook until tender, stirring occasionally. Add
spinach; cook just until wilted. Stir in beans, tomatoes and seasonings;
heat through. To serve, divide bean mixture among 4 bowls. Top with
poached eggs and green onions, if desired. Makes 4 servings.

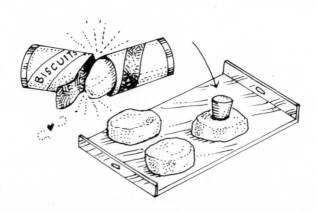

Doughnuts in a dash! For speedy homemade doughnuts,
separate refrigerated biscuits and cut a hole in the center
of each. Fry biscuits in hot oil until golden on both sides;
drain on paper towels. Roll in sugar and serve warm.

Breakfast Sunny-Side Up

Coffee Crumb Cake

Anne Alesauskas
Minocqua, WI

In our family, coffee cake is actually made with coffee! I loved this for breakfast when I was young and still love it now that I'm older.

3 c. all-purpose flour
1-1/2 c. sugar
4 t. baking powder
1 t. salt
1 t. nutmeg

2 t. cinnamon
2/3 c. chilled butter
2 eggs, beaten
1-1/3 c. brewed coffee, cooled
3/4 c. chopped pecans

In a large bowl, combine flour, sugar, baking powder, salt and spices. Mix well; cut in butter with a fork until crumbly. Set aside 3/4 cup of mixture for topping. Add eggs and coffee; stir until mixed well. Pour batter into a greased 13"x9" baking pan. Sprinkle with reserved crumb mixture and pecans. Bake at 350 degrees for 35 to 40 minutes. Serve warm. Makes 12 to 15 servings.

Country Fried Apples

Nancy Kaiser
York, SC

My family loves these apples! They're good with breakfast or brunch and it's great with supper too.

6 to 8 cooking apples, peeled, cored and sliced
1/2 to 3/4 c. brown sugar, packed

1 t. cinnamon
1/4 to 3/8 t. nutmeg
1/8 t. salt
2 to 3 T. red cinnamon candies

Combine all ingredients in a non-stick skillet; do not add any butter or oil. Stir gently. Cook, uncovered, over medium heat until apples are softened and tender, turning often, to desired consistency. Serves 6 to 8.

Keep apple pie spice on hand to use in all kinds of recipes. A blend of cinnamon, nutmeg and allspice, it's like a spice rack in a jar.

FRESH FARMHOUSE
Recipes

Ham, Spinach & Cheddar Bread Pudding

Gina McClenning
Nicholson, GA

Mom loved to make this savory bread pudding whenever we had weekend guests. It goes well when paired with breakfast potatoes, fruit and toast.

18-oz. loaf challah bread, cut into one-inch cubes and divided
2 c. cooked ham, diced and divided
1/4 c. butter
1 sweet onion, chopped
3 cloves garlic, minced
6-oz. pkg. fresh baby spinach

8-oz. pkg. shredded Cheddar cheese
5-oz. pkg. shredded Parmesan cheese
2 T. fresh thyme, minced
5 eggs, beaten
16-oz. container half-and-half
1/2 c. whole milk
1/4 c. Dijon mustard

Spread half of bread cubes evenly in a buttered 13"x9" baking pan. Top evenly with half of ham and set aside. In a large skillet, melt butter over medium heat. Add onion and cook for 3 to 4 minutes, until tender. Add garlic and sauté 2 minutes more. Add spinach and cook for 2 to 3 minutes, until wilted. Remove from heat. Spread half of spinach mixture evenly over ham in pan. In a bowl, combine cheeses and thyme. Sprinkle half of cheese mixture evenly over spinach mixture. In another bowl, whisk together eggs, half-and-half, milk and mustard. Pour half of egg mixture evenly over spinach mixture. Repeat layers with remaining bread, ham, spinach mixture, cheese mixture and egg mixture. Let stand for 30 minutes, pressing bread down lightly with the back of a wooden spoon. Bake, uncovered, at 350 degrees for 45 minutes to one hour, until center is set and top is golden. Let stand for 10 minutes before serving. Serves 8 to 10.

Pull out Grandma's vintage baking dishes...they're just right for baking hearty casseroles, with a side dish of nostalgia!

Breakfast Sunny-Side Up

Corned Beef Hash & Eggs

Gail Blain
Grand Island, NE

This is my favorite leftover recipe, hands-down! My family requests corned beef for dinner just so we can have hash for breakfast. In a pinch, you can use thick-sliced corned beef from the deli.

2 T. oil
1/2 lb. cooked corned beef, diced
1 white onion, finely chopped
1 green pepper, finely chopped
2 baking potatoes, peeled and
  grated

1/4 c. butter
4 eggs
salt and pepper to taste
4 slices Cheddar cheese

Heat oil in a medium skillet over high heat; add corned beef. Cook for about 3 minutes, stirring until beef releases some fat and browns lightly. Stir in onion, green pepper and potatoes. Cook without stirring for about 6 minutes, until crisp and golden on the bottom. Continue cooking for about 15 more minutes, turning hash as it browns evenly. Meanwhile, melt butter in a separate skillet over medium-high heat. Fry eggs over easy or sunny-side up (see page 36); season with salt and pepper. Arrange cheese slices on top of hash; reduce heat to low and let stand until cheese melts, about one minute. To serve, top each portion of hash with a fried egg. Serves 4.

Broiled tomatoes are a tasty, quick garnish for egg dishes. Place tomato halves on a broiler pan, cut-side up. Drizzle lightly with olive oil; season with salt and pepper. Broil tomatoes until tender, 2 to 3 minutes.

FRESH FARMHOUSE
Recipes

Rainbow Quiche

Joyceann Dreibelbis
Wooster, OH

Start the day with this super eye-opener! With plenty of veggies and a creamy egg & cheese filling, this tasty quiche gets two thumbs up.

9-inch deep-dish pie crust, unbaked
2 T. butter
1-1/2 c. broccoli flowerets, finely chopped
1 c. sliced mushrooms
1/2 c. onion, finely chopped
1/2 c. green pepper, finely chopped
1/2 c. red pepper, finely chopped
1/2 c. orange pepper, finely chopped
1 c. fresh spinach, chopped
1 c. shredded Mexican-blend cheese
6 eggs, beaten
1-3/4 c. whole or 2% milk
salt to taste

Arrange pie crust in a 9" deep-dish pie plate. Trim and flute edges; set aside. Melt butter in a large skillet over medium heat; sauté broccoli, mushrooms, onion and peppers until tender. Stir in spinach. Spoon into crust; sprinkle with cheese and set aside. In a large bowl, whisk together eggs, milk and salt; pour over cheese. Bake at 350 degrees for 45 to 55 minutes, until a knife tip inserted near the center comes out clean. Let stand for 10 minutes; cut into wedges. Makes 6 to 8 servings.

Eggs will beat up fluffier if they're at room temperature and not too cold. Set them out while preparing the rest of the dish, or slip eggs carefully into a bowl of lukewarm water and let stand for 15 minutes...they'll warm right up.

Breakfast Sunny-Side Up

Savory Cheese Muffins

Kathy Grashoff
Fort Wayne, IN

Yummy with breakfast or alongside a bowl of soup! Make them even better by adding some crumbled bacon.

1 c. plus 2 T. all-purpose flour
2 t. baking powder
1/4 t. salt
1/8 t. pepper
1 egg

1/4 c. olive oil
1/2 c. milk
3/4 t. dried dill weed
1 c. shredded extra-sharp
    Cheddar cheese

In a bowl, combine flour, baking powder, salt and pepper; set aside. Lightly beat egg in another bowl; stir in olive oil, milk and dill weed. Stir in cheese. Add egg mixture to flour mixture; stir with a fork until just combined. Divide batter evenly among 6 greased muffin cups. Bake at 450 degrees for about 8 to 10 minutes until golden and a toothpick comes out clean. Serve warm. Makes 6 muffins.

Spice up breakfast with cider-glazed sausages. Brown and drain 1/2 pound of breakfast sausage links. Add a cup of apple cider to the skillet, then turn the heat down to low and simmer for 10 minutes.

FRESH FARMHOUSE
Recipes

Breakfast Potatoes with Bacon
Dale Duncan
Waterloo, IA

Delicious alongside eggs done your favorite way.

3 slices peppered bacon
3 lbs. redskin potatoes, quartered

salt and pepper to taste
Garnish: sliced green onions

Cook bacon in a large skillet over medium-high heat, turning occasionally, until crisp. Remove bacon to paper towels, reserving drippings in skillet. Add potatoes to skillet. Cook over medium-high heat for 15 to 20 minutes, until crisp and golden on the outside and soft on the inside. Reduce heat if cooking too quickly. Season with salt and pepper. Garnish with crumbled bacon and green onions, if desired. Makes 6 servings.

The kiss of the sun for pardon,
The song of the birds for mirth;
One is nearer God's heart in a garden
Than anywhere else on earth.
–Dorothy Frances Gurney

Breakfast Sunny-Side Up

Old-Fashioned Buttermilk Biscuits

Joyce Roebuck
Jacksonville, TX

Nothing beats a good biscuit with sausage for breakfast!

2 c. all-purpose flour
4 t. baking powder
1/2 t. baking soda
1/2 t. salt

5 T. shortening
1 c. buttermilk
Garnish: melted butter or oil

In a large bowl, sift together flour, baking powder, baking soda and salt. Using a fork, cut in shortening to pea size. Add buttermilk all at once; stir until dough follows the fork around bowl. Turn dough onto a floured surface; knead about 30 seconds. Roll out dough 3/8-inch thick on floured surface. Cut out biscuits with a 2-inch biscuit cutter; place on ungreased baking sheets. Brush with melted butter or oil. Bake at 450 degrees for 12 to 15 minutes, until golden. Makes 10 to 12 biscuits.

No buttermilk? Stir one tablespoon vinegar or lemon juice into one cup milk and let stand for 5 minutes.

FRESH FARMHOUSE
Recipes

Eggs for Breakfast, 4 Ways

Eggs Sunny-Side Up or Over Easy

Break 2 to 3 eggs into a buttered skillet over medium-low heat. Cook until edges begin to set. Add a tablespoon of water; cover skillet and turn up the heat a little. Cook for one to 2 minutes more, until yolks are as done as you like. For eggs over easy, carefully turn eggs over when the edges set; finish cooking the same way.

Scrambled Eggs

Whisk together 2 to 3 eggs, one tablespoon milk per egg, salt and pepper to taste. Melt 2 teaspoons butter in a skillet over medium heat; pour in eggs. As eggs begin to set, pull gently across the pan with a pancake turner; do not stir constantly. Cook until eggs are thickened and lightly set.

Poached Eggs

Add 2 to 3 inches of water to a skillet; bring to a simmer over medium-high heat. Swirl the water with a spoon and gently slide in an egg from a saucer. Let cook until set, about 2 minutes; remove egg with a slotted spoon.

Soft-Boiled Eggs

Bring a large saucepan of water to a boil over medium-high heat. Carefully add several eggs. Cook for 6-1/2 minutes while gently boiling. Spoon eggs into a bowl of ice water and let stand for 2 minutes; drain and peel.

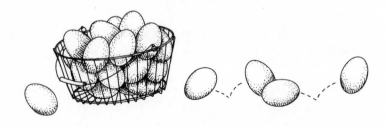

Nourishing Soups & Breads

Marta's Vegetable Soup

Marta Norton
Redlands, CA

There's nothing better on a cold day than soup! This chunky soup gets a punch of flavor from salsa and spices. I love to add a dollop of sour cream and a sprinkle of chopped cilantro on top.

3/4 c. red onion, coarsely chopped
4 cloves garlic, minced
1/2 lb. sliced mushrooms
2 to 3 t. olive oil
3/4 c. white wine or chicken broth
4 c. chicken broth
2 c. mild or medium salsa
1.35-oz. pkg. onion soup mix
3 to 4 T. chili powder, to taste
1 T. ground cumin, or to taste
2 yellow crookneck squash, coarsely chopped
2 zucchini, coarsely chopped
1 bunch asparagus, trimmed and coarsely chopped
1 head cabbage, coarsely chopped
1 red pepper, coarsely chopped
Optional: additional chicken broth

In a large stockpot over medium heat, sauté onion, garlic and mushrooms in oil until almost tender. Stir in 3/4 cup wine or chicken broth; continue to sauté until translucent. Add 4 cups chicken broth. Stir in salsa, onion soup mix and seasonings. Add remaining vegetables and stir well. Reduce heat to medium-low. Simmer until vegetables have cooked down, stirring occasionally. For a thinner consistency, add additional chicken broth as desired. Makes 8 to 10 servings.

When making soup, slice vegetables into same-size pieces before you begin cooking...they'll all be done to perfection at the same time.

Nourishing Soups & Breads

Sausage & Corn Chowder

Bethi Hendrickson
Danville, PA

*This quick and filling soup will remind you of supper at Mom's house!
Served with a tossed salad and crusty bread, it's sure to quickly
become a family favorite.*

16-oz. pkg. Italian pork sausage
   link, casing removed
2 T. olive oil
1 c. onion, finely chopped
1 red pepper, finely chopped
3 to 4 redskin potatoes, cubed

2 15-1/4 oz. cans corn, drained
2 c. chicken broth
1/4 c. all-purpose flour
2 c. milk
dried parsley and pepper to taste

Crumble sausage into a large skillet. Cook over medium heat for about
5 minutes, until browned; drain. Remove from heat. Meanwhile, in a
large saucepan over medium heat, combine oil, onion, red pepper and
potatoes. Cover and cook for 5 minutes; stir in corn and chicken broth.
In a bowl, whisk together flour and milk until smooth. Add flour mixture
to skillet; return sausage to skillet. Season with parsley and pepper. Add
sausage mixture to corn mixture. Simmer over medium-low heat for
15 minutes, or until potatoes are fork-tender. Makes 6 to 8 servings.

Just for fun, bake your next batch of cornbread in
an old-fashioned corn stick pan...the kind that makes
cornbread sticks shaped like ears of corn.
Kids will love 'em!

FRESH FARMHOUSE
Recipes

Tomato-Celery Soup

Mary Ann McGrath
Lawrenceburg, KY

*This is my version of a Shaker recipe from nearby Pleasant Hill.
It is served in the Inn at Shakertown in Kentucky. It is quick &
easy to make and tastes delicious!*

1/4 c. butter
1 c. onion, finely chopped
1 c. celery, finely chopped
23.2-oz. can tomato soup
2-3/4 c. water

2 T. lemon juice
1 T. sugar
1-1/2 t. fresh parsley, minced
1/2 t. salt
1/4 t. pepper

Melt butter in a large saucepan over medium heat. Add onion and
celery; cook until onion is transparent. Stir in remaining ingredients and
bring to a boil. Reduce heat to low; simmer for 5 to 10 minutes. Makes
8 servings.

Fresh Herb Spoon Rolls

Laura Fuller
Fort Wayne, IN

These warm morsels of fresh bread are wonderful anytime.

1-1/4 oz. pkg. active dry yeast
1/4 c. sugar
2 c. very warm water, about
    110 to 115 degrees
4 c. self-rising flour

3/4 c. butter, melted
1 egg, lightly beaten
1/4 c. fresh chives, chopped
1/2 c. fresh parsley, chopped

In a large bowl, combine yeast, sugar and warm water. Stir; let stand
for 5 minutes. Fold in remaining ingredients, mixing well. Spoon batter
into 24 lightly greased muffin cups. Bake at 400 degrees for 20 to
22 minutes, until golden. Makes 2 dozen.

Use a damp brush sprinkled with
baking soda to scrub fruits &
veggies...no fancy produce
wash needed!

Nourishing Soups & Breads

Nana's Potato Soup

Debbie Dunham
Lumberton, TX

*Whether it's chilly outside or you're feeling under the weather,
this soup always hits the spot! Delicious as is, or topped
with cheese, sour cream and bacon bits...yum!*

8 to 12 redskin potatoes, peeled
 and diced
1/2 c. yellow onion, diced
1/2 c. yellow or orange pepper,
 diced
Optional: 1/2 lb. mushrooms,
 diced

1 to 1-1/2 t. salt
1 c. chicken broth
1 c. milk
1-1/2 c. fresh kale, chopped

In a large soup pot, combine potatoes, onion, pepper and mushrooms,
if using. Add enough water to cover vegetables by one to 2 inches; add
one teaspoon salt. Bring to a boil over high heat; reduce heat to low
and simmer for about 20 minutes. Add chicken broth, milk and chopped
kale. Bring to a low boil and simmer until potatoes are mushy. Season
with remaining salt, if needed. Makes 8 servings.

At farmers' markets and even at the supermarket, watch for
heirloom vegetables...varieties that Grandma might have grown
in her garden. These veggies don't always look picture-perfect,
but their flavor can't be beat!

Chicken-Veggie Soup with Lemon & Dill

Beth Backer
Cleveland, OH

To me, soup is a perfect comfort food. I'm a recently diagnosed diabetic looking for good things I can eat...this really fills the bill. Using a slow cooker makes this easy-peasy!

3/4 c. yellow onion, chopped
1 celery, chopped
1 carrot, peeled and chopped
2 T. olive oil
3 cloves garlic, minced
3 boneless, skinless chicken
   breasts, cubed
6 c. chicken broth
1 t. dried parsley

1/2 t. dried dill weed
1/4 t. dried basil
salt and pepper to taste
zest and juice of 1 lemon
1 lemon, sliced
1 zucchini, spiralized or cut
   into matchsticks
2 c. fresh baby spinach

In a skillet over medium heat, sauté onion, celery and carrot in oil for about 5 minutes, until softened. Add garlic; cook for one more minute. Transfer onion mixture to a 6-quart slow cooker. Add chicken, chicken broth, seasonings, lemon zest, juice and sliced lemon. Cover and cook on low setting for 8 to 10 hours, or on high setting for 4 to 6 hours. In the last hour of cooking, add zucchini; add spinach in the last 30 minutes. Serves 6.

Homemade croutons are simple to make...delicious on soups and salads. Melt 1/4 cup butter in a skillet over medium heat. Stir in 3 cups of bread cubes and toss to coat. Cook, stirring occasionally, until crisp and golden and crisp. A great way to use up day-old bread!

Nourishing Soups & Breads

Green Garden Soup

Regina Wickline
Pebble Beach, CA

This creamy soup tastes like springtime! Perfect with a chicken salad sandwich, or ladle it into cups as a dinner starter.

1 T. olive oil
1 lb. asparagus, trimmed and
   cut into 1-inch pieces
2 stalks celery with some leaves,
   chopped
1/2 c. onion, chopped
1/4 c. long-cooking rice,
   uncooked

1 t. dried oregano
1/2 t. dried thyme
14-1/2 oz. can chicken or
   vegetable broth
1 c. water
6 fresh spinach leaves, chopped
Optional: sour cream, fresh dill

Heat oil in a large saucepan over medium heat. Add asparagus, celery and onion; cook until softened, about 5 minutes. Stir in uncooked rice and seasonings; add broth and water. Bring to a boil; reduce heat to low. Cover and simmer for 15 minutes. Working in batches as needed, pour soup into a blender and process until smooth; return to saucepan. Return to a simmer; stir in spinach and cook for 2 to 3 minutes. Garnish with sour cream and dill, if desired. Serves 4.

Fresh herbs will last a week or more if you snip off
the stem ends, arrange them in a tall glass with an inch
of water and cover loosely with a plastic bag.

FRESH FARMHOUSE
Recipes

Polish Cabbage Soup

Doreen Knapp
Stanfordville, NY

This was my mom's and aunt's recipe...I miss them both so very much. It's one of my go-to meals every fall through winter. The Kielbasa can be replaced with browned Italian sausage...both ways are tasty! Serve with a loaf of crusty bread on the side.

1 t. olive oil, divided
1 c. yellow onion, chopped
3 carrots, peeled and diced
3 stalks celery, chopped
1 lb. Kielbasa sausage, chopped
3 32-oz. containers beef broth
2 28-oz. cans diced tomatoes

1 t. onion powder
1 t. garlic powder
1 t. fennel seed
1 t. pepper
2 bay leaves
1/2 head cabbage, shredded

Heat oil in a soup pot over medium heat; add onion, carrots and celery. Sauté until onion is translucent, about 3 to 5 minutes. Add Kielbasa and sauté until golden. Add beef broth; scrape the bottom of the pot and stir well. Add tomatoes with juice and stir well. Add seasonings and stir well. Reduce heat to medium-low; simmer for about one hour. Stir in cabbage and simmer until tender, 30 to 45 minutes. Discard bay leaves before serving. Serves 6.

A flexible plastic cutting mat makes speedy work of slicing & dicing. After chopping, just fold it in half and pour ingredients into the mixing bowl.

Nourishing Soups & Breads

Garden Tomato Soup

Stephanie D'Esposito
Ravena, NY

My dad taught me how to make this fresh tomato soup and it is so delicious. Every summer, my garden produces an abundance of tomatoes. I use them to make this soup and freeze it, then thaw it to enjoy in the fall. It's wonderful!

8 lbs. ripe tomatoes
1 T. salt
5 cloves garlic, peeled
12-oz. can tomato paste
2 T. sugar
salt to taste

1 t. pepper
1/4 c. fresh basil, chopped
1 c. half-and-half
Garnish: shredded mozzarella
   cheese

Quarter enough tomatoes to fill an a 8-quart slow cooker. Using your hands, squeeze tomatoes to release the juice. Add salt and garlic. Cover and cook on high setting for 4 hours, or until tomatoes and garlic are broken down. Working in batches, process tomato mixture through a food mill, catching the juice in a large bowl. Discard tomato pulp, skins and seeds; return juice to slow cooker. Stir in tomato paste, sugar, salt to taste, pepper and basil. Cover and cook on low setting for one hour. Stir in half-and-half; cover and warm through. Serve with a sprinkle of mozzarella cheese. Makes 6 to 8 servings.

Sweet Potato Biscuits

Jen Stout
Brandon, PA

Serve with butter and honey...yum!

1 c. sweet potatoes, peeled,
   cooked and mashed
1 T. butter, room temperature
1 T. sugar

1/2 t. baking soda
1/3 c. buttermilk
2 c. all-purpose flour
1 t. salt

In a bowl, beat sweet potatoes, butter and sugar until blended. In a separate bowl, dissolve baking soda in buttermilk; add potato mixture and mix well. Combine flour and salt; add to potato mixture and mix well. Roll out dough on a floured surface to 1/2-inch thick. Cut with a biscuit cutter; arrange on a greased baking sheet. Bake at 400 degrees for 15 to 20 minutes, until golden. Makes about one dozen.

FRESH FARMHOUSE
Recipes

Hamburger Vegetable Soup

Crystal Willich
Horton, KS

*So delicious on a cold wintry night...or any time
you're just really hungry!*

1 lb. ground beef
3/4 c. onion, diced
3 c. chicken broth
4 c. cocktail vegetable juice
4 c. tomato juice
28-oz. can diced tomatoes
2 to 3 potatoes, peeled and diced
2 to 3 carrots, peeled and sliced
   or diced

3 to 4 stalks celery with leaves,
   sliced
1/2 head cabbage, shredded
1 t. salt
1/2 t. pepper
Optional: additional tomato juice,
   salt and pepper
10-oz. pkg. frozen peas

Brown beef with onion in a soup pot over medium heat; drain. Add
chicken broth, both juices, tomatoes with juice, potatoes, carrots, celery,
cabbage, salt and pepper. Bring to a boil; reduce heat to medium-low
and simmer until vegetables are nearly tender. For a thinner consistency,
add more tomato juice; season with more salt and pepper, if needed. Stir
in frozen peas and cook 5 minutes longer. Makes 8 servings.

Stir some quick-cooking alphabet macaroni into a pot
of vegetable soup...kids of all ages will love it!

Nourishing Soups & Breads

Cheesy Broccoli Noodle Soup

Janice Woods
Northern Cambrian, PA

A satisfying soup...noodles make it different from the usual broccoli soup. Serve with hard rolls.

3/4 c. onion, chopped
2 T. butter
6 c. water
6 cubes chicken bouillon
6 c. milk
8-oz. pkg. fine egg noodles, uncooked

16-oz. pkg. pasteurized process cheese, cubed
2 t. garlic powder
1 t. pepper
2 10-oz. pkgs. frozen chopped broccoli, thawed

In a large soup pot over medium heat, sauté onion in butter for about 3 minutes. Add water and bouillon cubes; bring to a boil. Stir in milk and uncooked noodles; add cheese, garlic powder and pepper. Simmer over medium-low to medium heat for about 12 minutes, until cheese melts and noodles are tender, stirring occasionally. Add broccoli; cook for 10 minutes more. Makes 8 to 10 servings.

On the way to the farmers' market, watch for clever places to take snapshots out in the country. How about the whole family lined up in front of a cornfield or a big round hay bale? Later, photos can be turned into delightful holiday cards.

FRESH FARMHOUSE
Recipes

Borsch

Lovie Daily
Manitoba, Canada

This recipe for beet soup with vegetables has been in our family for generations. We like to add the cut-up beet leaves and stems for flavor. Top with a drizzle of cream, if you like.

16 c. water
3 beets, peeled and shredded
2 c. canned stewed tomatoes
1.4-oz. pkg. vegetable soup mix
1 c. carrots, peeled and diced
1 c. yellow or green beans
1 c. cabbage, shredded

1/4 c. peas
1/4 c. corn
3 T. white vinegar
salt to taste
1 c. ribbon egg noodles,
    uncooked
1/4 c. whipping cream

In a large soup pot over medium-high heat, combine water, beets, tomatoes and soup mix; bring to a boil. Add remaining vegetables; vinegar and salt to taste. For a thinner consistency, add more water. Reduce heat to medium-low. Simmer for one hour, stirring occasionally, or until vegetables are tender. Stir in uncooked noodles; simmer for 10 to 12 minutes, until cooked. Stir in cream and serve. Makes 10 servings.

Keep fresh beets from staining your hands while cutting them...rub your hands with vegetable oil first.

Sausage & Lentil Stew

Eleanor Dionne
Beverly, MA

We love this recipe, it's hearty and so good! I make this when it's cold outside. Serve with a loaf of country-style bread.

2 T. olive oil
12-oz. pkg. Italian pork sausage
   links, removed from casings
   and crumbled
3/4 c. carrots, peeled and
   finely chopped
1 c. onion, finely chopped
4 cloves garlic, minced

coarse salt and pepper to taste
2 T. tomato paste
3 c. chicken broth
3 c. water
1 c. dried brown lentils, rinsed
   and sorted
Optional: 1/2 c. kale, finely
   chopped

Heat oil in a large pot over medium-high heat. Add crumbled sausage, carrots, onion and garlic. Cook and stir until sausage is no longer pink, about 5 minutes; drain. Season with salt and pepper. Stir in tomato paste; cook and stir for one minute. Add chicken broth, water and lentils; bring to a boil. Reduce heat to low. Cover and simmer for about 30 minutes, until lentils are tender. If desired, add kale; cook and stir until wilted. Makes 4 servings.

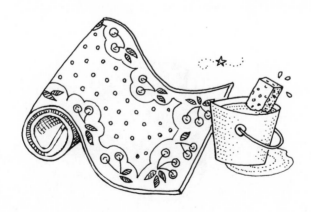

Brightly colored vintage-style oilcloth makes the best-ever tablecloth...it wipes clean in a jiffy!

FRESH FARMHOUSE
Recipes

Chicken Chili Soup

Lisa Gowen
Saint Charles, MO

A group of our friends had a chili get-together. This recipe is the one my husband loved!

2 T. oil
2-1/2 lbs. boneless, skinless
   chicken, cubed
2 c. celery, chopped
1-1/2 c. onion, chopped
4 cloves garlic, minced
2 15-oz. cans tomato sauce
14-1/2 oz. can stewed tomatoes,
   cut up
1 c. chicken broth

1 red pepper, chopped
2 T. chili powder, or to taste
1 T. sugar
1 t. dried basil
1/2 t. dried oregano
1/2 t. ground cumin
1/2 t. red pepper flakes
1 bay leaf
1/2 lb. sliced mushrooms

Heat oil in a large soup pot over medium heat. Add chicken, celery, onion and garlic; cook until chicken is golden and vegetables are tender. Stir in tomato sauce, tomatoes with juice and chicken broth; bring to a boil. Reduce heat to medium-low. Cover and simmer for 15 minutes. Stir in seasonings; cover and simmer another 30 minutes. Stir in mushrooms; cook for another 10 minutes. Discard bay leaf and serve. Makes 6 to 8 servings.

Have fun with chili toppers. Set out a selection for guests
to choose from...diced avocado, sliced jalapeño peppers,
shredded Mexican-style cheese and cool sour cream.
Add some crushed tortilla chips for crunch!

Cheddar Chowder

Diana Krol
Hutchinson, KS

This chowder is the perfect answer to take the chill out of the evening...but really, it's good anytime. It's quick to make, the ingredients are all at hand and it's delicious!

2 c. potatoes, peeled and diced
1/2 c. carrots, peeled and diced
1/2 c. celery, diced
1/4 c. onion, diced
2 c. water
1 t. salt

1/4 t. pepper
Optional: 1 c. cooked ham, diced
Garnish: bacon crumbles,
    chopped green onion,
    additional shredded cheese

In a soup pot over medium-high heat, combine vegetables, water, salt and pepper; bring to a boil. Reduce heat to medium and simmer for 10 to 12 minutes, until tender. Meanwhile, make White Sauce; pour over tender vegetables and stir well. Add ham, if desired; heat through but do not boil. Garnish as desired. Makes 4 servings.

White Sauce:

1/4 c. butter
1/4 c. all-purpose flour
2 c. milk

8-oz. pkg. shredded Cheddar
    cheese

In a large saucepan over medium heat, melt butter. Stir in flour until a paste forms. Blend in milk; cook and stir until thickened. Fold in cheese; cook and stir until melted.

Embellish a small notebook with seed packet clippings... useful for keeping schedules, or making a list for your next visit to the farmers' market!

FRESH FARMHOUSE
Recipes

Turkey & Sweet Potato Soup
Nikki Bradshaw
Kinderhook, IL

This satisfying slow-cooker soup is chock-full of veggies!
It's a great way to use leftover holiday turkey.

4 c. turkey or chicken broth
1 c. sweet potato, peeled and
   cut into 1-inch cubes
15.8-oz. can Great Northern
   beans, drained and rinsed
14-1/2 oz. can cut green beans,
   drained
4-oz. can sliced mushrooms,
   drained

2 carrots, peeled and sliced
1 to 2 stalks celery, sliced
1/2 c. onion, diced
2 cloves garlic, minced
salt and pepper to taste
dried thyme to taste
1 to 1-1/2 c. cooked turkey,
   cubed or shredded
1 c. frozen peas, rinsed

Add all ingredients except turkey and peas to a 6-quart slow cooker;
stir to combine. Cover and cook on low setting for 6 to 8 hours, until
vegetables are tender. During the last 30 minutes, stir in turkey and
peas; heat through. Makes 6 to 8 servings.

Crunchy tortilla strips are tasty soup toppers. Cut corn
tortillas into thin strips, then deep-fry quickly and drain
on paper towels. Try red or blue tortillas for variety.

Nourishing
Soups & Breads

Hearty Butternut Squash Soup

Joanne Mauseth
Clear Lake, SD

*A delicious soup for a chilly fall day. Spice it up
by using a hotter pepper!*

1 lb. Italian pork sausage link,
  skin removed
1 onion, diced
1 red pepper, diced
1 butternut squash, peeled
  and cubed
4 cloves garlic, minced
4 c. water

5 cubes chicken bouillon
2 15-1/2 oz. cans pinto or
  navy beans, drained
14-1/4 oz. can corn, drained
1 t. salt
1/8 t. pepper
Garnish: sour cream, chopped
  fresh cilantro

Crumble sausage into a stockpot over medium heat; add onion and red
pepper. Cook until sausage is browned and vegetables are tender; drain.
Add squash, garlic, water and bouillon cubes; bring to a boil. Reduce
heat to medium-low. Simmer until squash is very tender, stirring
occasionally. Gently mash squash in pan. Stir in beans, corn, salt and
pepper; simmer for 15 minutes. Garnish servings with sour cream and
cilantro. Makes 4 servings.

The art of being happy lies in the power of
extracting happiness from common things.
–Henry Ward Beecher

FRESH FARMHOUSE
Recipes

Lori's Snowstorm Potato Soup

Lori Richards
South Marysville, OH

One night, it was snowing like crazy and we didn't want to go out for dinner. I tossed this together and we all enjoyed it.

2 T. butter
1 c. carrots, peeled and sliced
1 c. celery, sliced
1/2 c. onion, diced
32-oz. container chicken or
    vegetable broth
1 lb. potatoes, peeled and diced

1/2 c. milk
1 T. all-purpose flour
1/2 t. salt, or to taste
1/2 t. pepper, or to taste
Optional: shredded Cheddar
    cheese, sliced green onions

Melt butter in a Dutch oven over medium heat. Sauté carrots, celery and onion until onion is translucent. Add chicken broth; simmer for 10 minutes. Add potatoes and simmer another 10 minutes, or until potatoes are soft. Add milk and flour; whisk well until broth thickens. Season with salt and pepper as desired. Top servings with cheese and onions, if desired. Makes 4 generous servings.

Keep a few quart-size Mason jars tucked in the cupboard so you can send home some homemade soup with a dinner guest...what a thoughtful gesture!

Nourishing Soups & Breads

Cream of Celery Soup

Jennifer Noemi
Nova Scotia, Canada

Creamy and comforting...old-fashioned goodness!

3 c. onion, coarsely chopped
2 T. olive oil
6 c. vegetable broth
8 c. celery, chopped
1 t. celery seed

3/4 t. dried summer savory
1/4 t. pepper
2 c. milk
1/3 c. whipping cream

In a large saucepan over medium heat, cook onion in olive oil until soft and translucent, about 10 minutes. Add vegetable broth, celery and seasonings. Bring to a boil; reduce heat to medium-low. Cover and simmer for 40 to 45 minutes, until celery is tender. Let cool slightly. Working in batches, purée mixture in a blender; return to saucepan. Stir in milk and cream; heat through, but do not allow to boil. Serves 6 to 8.

No-Knead Rustic Bread

Geneva Rogers
Gillette, WY

This recipe makes two tasty loaves...one to keep and one to share!

3 c. very warm water, about
    110 to 115 degrees
1-1/2 T. active dry yeast

1-1/2 T. coarse salt
6-1/2 c. all-purpose flour
1/2 c. cornmeal

In a large bowl, combine water, yeast and salt. Stir until mixture is foamy, about 10 minutes. Stir in flour until well blended; dough will be loose and look wet. Cover bowl loosely with a damp towel; let rise for about 5 hours. Sprinkle cornmeal over a large baking sheet. Shape dough into 2 loaves; place on baking sheet. Score tops several times with a serrated knife. Allow loaves to double in size, 30 to 60 minutes. Spray loaves lightly with water; bake at 425 degrees for about 20 minutes, until golden. Makes 2 loaves.

Get rid of tomato sauce stains on a plastic refrigerator container... simply rub the stain with a damp cloth dipped in baking soda.

FRESH FARMHOUSE
Recipes

Chilled Tomato & Fresh Basil Soup

Sharon Jones
Oklahoma City, OK

A good way to use up all those tomatoes in the garden...refreshing anytime!

2 lbs. ripe tomatoes, cored
2 T. onion
3 T. extra-virgin olive oil
2 to 3 T. red wine vinegar or
   balsamic vinegar, divided

salt and cracked pepper to taste
1/4 c. fresh basil, finely sliced
Garnish: additional olive oil

Add tomatoes and onion to a blender; purée until smooth. If desired, strain to remove bits of tomato skin; add mixture to a large bowl. Stir in olive oil, 2 tablespoons vinegar, salt and pepper. More vinegar may be added to taste, if desired. Cover and chill for one hour or more. At serving time, ladle into bowls and top with a sprinkle of basil. Garnish with a drizzle of olive oil and serve. Serves 4 to 6.

Take your family with you to the farmstand. Kids will love seeing all there is to enjoy...and a taste of juicy peach or warm tomato is a real treat!

Nourishing Soups & Breads

Cool-as-a-Cucumber Soup

Gladys Kielar
Whitehouse, OH

Enjoy this soup on a hot summer day. The dill and cucumbers make a great flavor combination.

1 lb. cucumbers, peeled, seeded
   and sliced
1/2 t. salt
1-1/2 c. fat-free plain yogurt
1 green onion, coarsely chopped

1 clove garlic, minced
4-1/2 t. fresh dill, snipped
Garnish: additional chopped
   green onions, snipped
   fresh dill

Set a colander in the sink. Add cucumbers; sprinkle with salt and toss. Let stand for 30 minutes. Rinse cucumbers; drain well and pat dry. Add cucumbers, yogurt, onion, and garlic to a food processor. Process until smooth; stir in dill. Serve immediately in chilled bowls, topped with additional onions and dill. Serves 6.

Chilled Gazpacho

Emilie Britton
New Bremen, OH

A classic cool soup...so easy to make.

4 c. tomato juice
1/2 c. French salad dressing
1/2 c. cucumber, chopped

1/2 c. onion, chopped
1/2 c. green pepper, chopped
Garnish: croutons

In a large bowl, mix together all ingredients except garnish; cover and chill. Serve topped with croutons. Serves 4.

Quick herb butter to serve with fresh-baked bread...simply roll a stick of butter in freshly chopped herbs, slice and serve.

FRESH FARMHOUSE
Recipes

Cabbage Roll Soup

Mel Chencharick
Julian, PA

This very tasty slow-cooker soup will warm your tummy from the inside out! Quick & easy, without a lot of fuss.

1 lb. thick-sliced bacon
1 lb. ground beef
1 c. onion, diced
3 cloves garlic, minced
2/3 c. long-grain rice, uncooked
6 to 8 c. cabbage, chopped
5 to 6 c. beef broth
28-oz. can diced tomatoes

10-3/4 oz. can tomato soup
1-1/2 c. vegetable cocktail juice
2 T. tomato paste
1 T. Worcestershire sauce
1 t. paprika
1 t. dried thyme
salt and pepper to taste
Garnish: chopped fresh parsley

In a skillet over medium heat, cook bacon until crisp. Drain bacon on paper towels, reserving one tablespoon drippings in skillet. Crumble bacon and refrigerate. Brown beef with onion in reserved drippings over medium heat. Drain; transfer beef mixture to a 6 to 7-quart slow cooker. Add remaining ingredients except garnish and reserved bacon; stir to combine. Crock will be very full. Cover and cook on high setting for 3 to 4 hours, or on low setting for 6 to 7 hours, until rice is fully cooked. Stir in half of reserved bacon. Spoon into bowls; top with remaining bacon and parsley. Serves 10 to 12.

Stock the freezer with comforting home-cooked soups.
Ladled into plastic freezer containers, they freeze well for
up to 3 months. To serve, thaw overnight in the refrigerator.
A great way to enjoy fresh-picked flavor throughout the year!

Vegetable Barley Soup

Tori Willis
Champaign, IL

We love this meatless soup with grilled cheese sandwiches.
If you prefer, add everything to a slow cooker, cover and
cook on low setting for 6 to 8 hours.

1 onion, chopped
2 stalks celery, chopped
2 to 3 carrots, peeled and
   chopped
2 to 3 t. olive oil
14-1/2 oz. can petite diced
   tomatoes
8 c. vegetable broth
1 c. long-cooking barley,
   uncooked
15-oz. can garbanzo beans,
   drained and rinsed

1 zucchini, chopped
1 t. sugar
1 t. garlic powder
1 t. dried parsley
1 t. curry powder
1 t. paprika
1 t. seasoned salt
1/2 t. pepper
3 bay leaves
1 t. Worcestershire sauce
Optional: additional vegetable
   broth or water

In a large soup pot, sauté onion, celery and carrots in oil until tender.
Add tomatoes with juice and remaining ingredients; bring to a boil over
medium-high heat. Reduce heat to medium-low. Cover and simmer for
90 minutes, stirring occasionally. Soup will be very thick; stir in more
broth or water, if desired. Discard bay leaves before serving. Makes
8 servings.

It's easy to stretch a pot of soup to make a few more servings...
just add an extra can or 2 of tomatoes or beans. The soup
will be extra hearty, and no one will know the difference!

FRESH FARMHOUSE
Recipes

Pennsylvania Dutch
Chicken-Corn Soup

Kathy Blankenship
Flemingsburg, KY

*I've searched the internet and never found this one-of-a-kind recipe!
It was shared with us many years ago, when I was still living at home,
and comes from our former pastors who were from Pennsylvania.
I know it sounds unusual, but I guarantee it's delicious! I hope
everyone will love it as much as we always have.*

8 c. water	2 16-oz. cans seasoned
1/2 c. butter	pinto beans
2 to 3 T. salt	15-oz. can corn
1 T. chicken soup base	4 to 6 eggs, hard-boiled, peeled
4-lb. whole chicken	and chopped
4 to 6 potatoes, peeled and diced	Optional: small amount of sugar
1 sweet onion, diced	to taste
salt to taste	Garnish: saltine crackers

In a large stockpot, combine water, butter, salt and soup base; add
chicken. Bring to a boil over high heat; reduce heat to medium-low.
Simmer until chicken is cooked through, adding more water as needed.
Remove chicken to a platter, reserving 4 to 6 cups broth in stockpot. Cut
chicken into bite-size pieces, discarding bones and skin; return chicken
to reserved broth in stockpot. Meanwhile, in a large saucepan, cover
potatoes and onion with water; season with salt. Cook over medium-
high heat until potatoes are soft, but still hold their shape well. Drain;
add potato mixture to chicken mixture in stockpot. Stir in beans with
liquid, corn with liquid, chopped eggs and sugar, if using. Mix well
and heat through. Serve with saltine crackers. Serves 12 or more.

Get together with friends and neighbors for a soup supper. Invite
everyone to bring their favorite veggies and cook up a big pot of
hearty vegetable soup together. While the soup simmers, you can
catch up on conversation or play board games together...so cozy!

Nourishing Soups & Breads

Saint Anthony's Soup

Marcia Shaffer
Conneaut Lake, PA

*Always served with crusty bread on Saint Anthony's Day (June 13)
or any other time the kids ask for it.*

1/4 c. oil	2 leeks, sliced
1 c. long-cooking barley,	1/2 c. mushrooms, chopped
uncooked	1/2 c. fresh parsley, minced
7 c. water	salt and pepper to taste
1 cube chicken bouillon	1 bay leaf
3 carrots, peeled and grated	

Heat oil in a skillet over medium heat. Add barley; cook and stir for
2 minutes, or until golden. Add barley and remaining ingredients to a
4-quart slow cooker. Cover and cook on low setting for 8 hours. Discard
bay leaf before serving. Makes 4 to 6 servings.

Turnip Green Soup

Bessie Branyon
Birmingham, AL

*This recipe has been sent around the country and people love it! Like
other soups, it is even better the next day. Good with cornbread.*

1 lb. smoked pork sausage link,	2 to 3 15-1/2 oz. cans pinto
chopped	beans or black-eyed peas
16-oz. pkg. frozen chopped	1.4-oz. pkg. vegetable soup mix
turnip greens	2 to 3 T. hot pepper sauce
4 c. water, or more as needed	

Brown sausage in a soup pot over medium heat; drain. Add remaining
ingredients. Simmer over medium-low heat for 30 to 45 minutes,
stirring occasionally. Makes 6 to 8 servings.

Dress up homemade or brown & serve dinner rolls. Before
baking, brush the dough with a little beaten egg, then sprinkle
with sesame seed, dried rosemary or grated Parmesan cheese.

FRESH FARMHOUSE
Recipes

Creamy Chicken Gnocchi Soup
Debbie Adkins
Nicholasville, KY

This comforting soup comes together quickly, especially if you use a deli rotisserie chicken. I've also made it without chicken and it's just as good. For extra nutrition, add a handful of fresh spinach.

1 c. celery, diced
1 c. onion, diced
1/2 c. carrot, peeled and
   shredded
1/4 c. olive oil, butter or
   bacon drippings
1/4 c. all-purpose flour
4 c. chicken broth

1-1/2 t. garlic powder
1/4 t. salt
1/2 t. pepper
3 c. refrigerated potato gnocchi
   pasta, uncooked
2 c. cooked chicken, chopped
2 c. half-and-half

In a large saucepan over medium heat, sauté celery, onion and carrot in oil, butter or drippings for 5 minutes. Stir in flour and cook for one minute. Add chicken broth and seasonings; bring to a boil and gently stir in gnocchi. Boil for 4 minutes, stirring occasionally. Reduce heat to low; stir in chicken. Cover and simmer over low heat for 10 minutes. Stir in half-and-half and simmer for 2 minutes; do not boil. Serves 4 to 6.

It's easy to save leftover fresh herbs. Spoon chopped herbs into an ice cube tray, one tablespoon per cube. Cover with water and freeze. Frozen cubes can be dropped right into hot stews or soups for fresh flavor in a jiffy.

Nourishing Soups & Breads

Cabbage Patch Soup

Joyceann Dreibelbis
Wooster, OH

This is a slightly sweet and mildly zippy soup. It's healthy and so easy to fix!

1/2 lb. ground beef
1-1/2 c. onion, chopped
1/2 c. celery, sliced
2 c. water
14-1/2 oz. can stewed tomatoes
16-oz. can kidney beans,
    drained and rinsed

1 c. cabbage, shredded
1 t. chili powder
1/2 t. salt
Optional: hot mashed potatoes

Brown beef in a large saucepan over medium heat; drain. Add onion and celery; cook until tender. Add water, tomatoes with juice, beans, cabbage and seasonings; bring to a boil. Reduce heat to medium-low. Cover and simmer for 20 to 30 minutes, until cabbage is tender. Ladle into soup bowls; top each bowl with a scoop of mashed potatoes, if desired. Makes 4 to 6 servings.

When frying bacon, it's easy to prepare a few extra slices to tuck into the fridge. Combine with juicy slices of sun-ripened tomato, frilly lettuce and creamy mayonnaise for a fresh BLT sandwich...tomorrow's lunch is ready in a jiffy!

FRESH FARMHOUSE
Recipes

Roasted Fennel & Onion Soup *Courtney Stultz*
Weir, KS

Fennel is one of my favorite soothing comfort foods and I really love French onion soup. So, I decided to combine the two and it's now a family favorite. Roasting the vegetables enhances the flavor. You can serve this up puréed or leave it chunky! Save a few of the leafy green fennel tops to use as a garnish.

2 to 3 whole fennel bulbs
1 large onion, sliced
2 T. coconut oil, melted
2 cloves garlic, minced
1/2 t. dried oregano

1/2 t. dried thyme
1 t. sea salt
1/2 t. pepper
3 to 4 c. chicken or beef broth

Slice the green stalks off fennel bulbs and discard; chop bulbs. Scatter fennel and onion on an aluminum foil-lined baking sheet. Drizzle with coconut oil; sprinkle with garlic and seasonings. Bake at 375 degrees for about 30 to 40 minutes, until vegetables are soft and lightly golden. Transfer vegetables to a large saucepan over low-medium heat; add broth. Cook until broth is warmed through. Serve as is, or for a smooth consistency, blend in pan using an immersion blender. Makes 4 servings.

Place onions in the freezer for just 5 minutes, then chop with an extra-sharp knife...no more tears!

Nourishing Soups & Breads

Cheesy Cauliflower Soup

Constance Bockstoce
Dallas, GA

This soup is a healthy and delicious way to eat more vegetables.
Loved by adults and children alike...a real comfort food.

1 head cauliflower, cut into
    flowerets
4 carrots, peeled and cut
    into bite-size pieces
2 T. dried celery flakes
2 t. no-salt herb seasoning

3 c. chicken broth
2 T. cornstarch
2 c. milk
8-oz. pkg. pasteurized process
    cheese, cubed, or
    1 c. shredded Cheddar cheese

In a large stockpot over medium heat, combine cauliflower, carrots, celery, herb seasoning and chicken broth. Cook for 20 minutes, or until tender, stirring occasionally. In a small bowl, mix cornstarch into milk. Pour into stockpot; cook and stir until thickened. Fold in cheese; stir until melted. Makes 4 to 6 servings.

Cornmeal Chive Biscuits

Nancy Wise
Little Rock, AR

We love these tender biscuits with soup.

2 c. self-rising flour
1/2 c. self-rising cornmeal mix
1/2 c. cold butter, thickly sliced

1/3 c. fresh chives, chopped
1-1/4 c. buttermilk
2 T. butter, melted

Combine flour and cornmeal in a large bowl. Sprinkle with butter slices and toss. Cut in butter with a pastry blender until crumbly. Cover and chill for 10 minutes. Stir in chives. Add buttermilk, stirring just until moistened. Turn dough out onto a floured surface. Knead 3 or 4 times, gradually adding additional flour if needed. With floured hands, pat dough into a 9-inch by 5-inch rectangle, 3/4-inch thick; dust with flour. Fold dough over itself in 3 sections, starting with one short end. Repeat 2 more times; pat dough to 1/2-inch thickness. Cut with a 2-inch biscuit cutter. Place biscuits side-by-side on a lightly greased 15"x10" jelly-roll pan. Bake at 425 degrees for 13 to 15 minutes, until lightly golden. Remove from oven; brush with melted butter. Makes 2 dozen.

FRESH FARMHOUSE
Recipes

Creamy Comfort Chicken
Noodle Soup

Michelle Cook
Paris, AR

Comfort in a bowl! Whenever someone in the family has a cold,
I like to add some chopped hot peppers to the soup along with
the other veggies. It helps clear your sinuses!

4 boneless, skinless chicken
   breasts
6-1/2 c. chicken broth, divided
2 t. olive oil
4 carrots, peeled and chopped
4 celery stalks, chopped
1 onion, chopped
1/2 t. garlic powder

1/2 t. dried thyme
1/2 t. dried rosemary
1 t. kosher salt
1/2 t. pepper
12-oz. pkg. extra-wide egg
   noodles, uncooked
1 c. sliced mushrooms
1 c. whipping cream

Place chicken breasts in a skillet over medium heat; add 1/2 cup chicken broth. Cook until chicken is golden and juices run clear; set aside to cool. Meanwhile, in a large stockpot, heat olive oil over medium heat. Add carrots, celery and onion; sauté until tender. Add seasonings. Cut chicken into cubes; add to stockpot along with remaining broth. Simmer over medium-low heat for 20 minutes. Add uncooked noodles. Cook for an additional 15 minutes, or just until noodles are tender. Add mushrooms and cream. Simmer over low heat to desired thickness; do not boil. Serves 8.

Vintage tea towels are perfect for lining bread baskets. They'll keep freshly baked rolls toasty warm and add a dash of color to the table.

Nourishing
Soups & Breads

Split Pea & Holiday Ham Soup

Pat Martin
Riverside, CA

*Leftover holiday ham bones and scraps never go to waste
since I created this simple and delicious soup recipe.
Everyone has loved it! It freezes well too.*

1 lb. split peas, rinsed and sorted
1 meaty ham bone
1 to 2 c. cooked ham, diced
2 to 3 stalks celery, sliced
2 to 5 carrots, peeled and sliced
2 to 3 potatoes, peeled and diced

1 c. onion, diced
1/2 to t. onion salt
1/2 to t. garlic salt
1/2 t. dried thyme
1 t. pepper, or to taste

Add dried peas, ham bone and diced ham to a large Dutch oven; add
enough water to half-fill pan. Cover and bring to a boil over high heat;
reduce heat to medium-low. Simmer for about one hour until peas
soften, stirring occasionally. Add vegetables, seasonings and enough
water to fill pan; return to a boil. Simmer over low heat until peas and
vegetables are tender, about one to 2 hours, stirring occasionally.
Serves 10 to 12.

When fate hands you a lemon,
make lemonade.
–Dale Carnegie

FRESH FARMHOUSE
Recipes

Easy Cabbage Soup

Joanne Novellino
Bayville, NJ

I love to make this soup and freeze it in quart containers. It's so handy to thaw a container and reheat for a quick meal with a sandwich.

1 c. onion, chopped
2 cloves garlic, minced
2 T. butter
2 T. olive oil
46-oz. can tomato juice

15-oz. can low-sodium chicken
broth
16-oz. pkg. shredded
coleslaw mix
pepper to taste

In a soup pot over medium heat, sauté onion and garlic in butter and oil just until golden. Add remaining ingredients. Simmer over medium-low heat for about 1-1/2 hours, until cabbage is tender and melts into the soup. If consistency is too thick, add a little water or more broth. Makes 2 to 3 quarts.

Wild Rice Soup

Vicki Van Donselaar
Cedar, IA

With this easy recipe, it's easy to stir up enough hearty soup for a crowd. I always make a double batch, because it freezes and reheats so well.

2 c. water
1/2 c. wild rice, uncooked
1 t. salt
9 slices bacon
3/4 c. onion, chopped
1-1/2 c. milk

4 c. half-and-half, or 3 13-oz.
cans evaporated milk
2 10-3/4 oz. cans cream of
potato soup
2 c. pasteurized process cheese,
cubed

Bring water to a boil in a medium saucepan over high heat; reduce to medium-high. Add rice and salt; cook for 45 to 60 minutes, until rice is tender. Meanwhile, in a skillet over medium heat, cook bacon until crisp. Remove bacon to paper towels; reserve drippings in pan. Add onion to drippings and sauté until tender. In a large, heavy saucepan, combine drained rice, crumbled bacon, drained onion and remaining ingredients. Stir well. Cook over low heat until cheese melts; do not boil. Makes 6 to 8 servings.

Nourishing Soups & Breads

Chicken & Tomato Tortellini Soup

Tiffany Jones
Evansville, AR

My twins' three-year pics were taken on a cold day. After we were finished, we went to my cousin's house to visit and she fixed this soup for us. Such a comforting, delicious soup to warm you up!

14-oz. can chicken broth
14-1/2 oz. can diced tomatoes
14-1/2 can diced tomatoes with green chiles
15-1/2 oz. can red beans, drained

4-oz. can green chiles
1 c. cooked chicken, shredded
8-oz. pkg. cream cheese, cubed
9-oz. pkg. frozen cheese tortellini, uncooked

In a large soup pot over medium heat, combine chicken broth, tomatoes with juice, beans, chiles and chicken. Cook, stirring often, until heated through. Stir in cream cheese and tortellini. Simmer for 5 minutes, or until cream cheese is blended and tortellini is tender. Makes 6 servings.

Grilled cheese sandwiches go great with a bowl of soup.
Toast sandwiches on a waffle iron instead of a griddle...
kids will love 'em!

FRESH FARMHOUSE
Recipes

Vegetable & Sausage Stew

Amy Thomson Hunt
Traphill, NC

On chilly autumn evenings, this slow-cooker stew is
even better with a pan of broccoli cornbread on the side.

4 to 6 T. zesty Italian salad
   dressing
1-1/2 T. Dijon mustard
3 to 4 redskin potatoes, sliced
1 c. onion, sliced
1/2 c. celery, finely diced
1/2 c. green pepper, finely diced

2 c. cabbage, chopped
1-1/2 c. baby carrots
1 lb. turkey Kielbasa sausage,
   cut into 1-inch slices
14-1/2 oz. can Italian-seasoned
   diced tomatoes
salt and pepper to taste

In a small bowl, combine salad dressing and mustard; set aside. Layer
potatoes in a 4-quart slow cooker; drizzle with 1/3 of dressing mixture.
Layer onion, celery and green pepper on top of potatoes; drizzle with
1/3 of dressing mixture. Top with cabbage and carrots; drizzle with
remaining dressing mixture. Add sliced sausage on top of vegetables;
pour tomatoes with juice evenly over sausage. Cover and cook on low
setting for 7 to 8 hours. Serves 6.

Want to add a little flavor boost to a pot of soup?
Just add a splash of cider vinegar, lemon juice
or Worcestershire sauce.

Nourishing Soups & Breads

Skillet Quick & Easy Cornbread

Cindy Williams
Greensboro, KY

This is great for any meal...especially good with a bowl of steaming Great Northern beans. I've made this recipe for many years. It's very quick to toss together, with little effort. I bake it in a hot cast-iron skillet greased with a little melted bacon drippings and it's perfect every time!

2 to 3 t. bacon drippings
1 egg, beaten
1 c. whole milk
1 c. self-rising cornmeal
1 c. self-rising flour
Optional: 11-oz. can corn,
    drained

Spread bacon drippings in a 9" to 10" cast-iron skillet. Heat skillet in a 450-degree oven for about 3 minutes. Meanwhile, beat egg in a bowl; gradually beat in milk. Add cornmeal and flour; mix just until combined. Fold in corn, if using. Pour batter into hot skillet. Bake at 450 degrees for about 15 minutes, until golden on top and sides begin to pull away from skillet. Cut into wedges. Serves 6 to 8.

Shake up your best cornbread recipe! Stir in some shredded Cheddar cheese, crisply cooked and crumbled bacon or diced green chiles.

FRESH FARMHOUSE
Recipes

Chicken & Barley Stew *Lisa Ann Panzino DiNunzio*
Vineland, NJ

This is such a warming, comforting, delicious stew!
It warms you through and through.

4 boneless, skinless chicken
  breasts
2 carrots, peeled and diced
2 stalks celery, diced
1 onion, sliced
1 clove garlic, minced
1 c. long-cooking pearl barley,
  uncooked

2 bay leaves
1/2 t. dried thyme
sea salt and pepper to taste
14-1/2 oz. can diced tomatoes
  with mild green chiles
6 c. low-sodium chicken broth
15-1/4 oz. can corn, drained

Coat a 6-quart slow cooker with non-stick vegetable spray. Layer
chicken breasts in slow cooker, then carrots, celery, onion and garlic.
Add barley on top of vegetables; add bay leaves and seasonings. Pour
in tomatoes with juice and chicken broth. Cover and cook on low setting
for 6 to 8 hours. During the last 30 minutes of cooking, remove chicken
to a platter and cool; discard bay leaves. Shred chicken breasts into
bite-size pieces and return to slow cooker; stir in corn. Gently stir soup
until heated through. Serves 4 to 6.

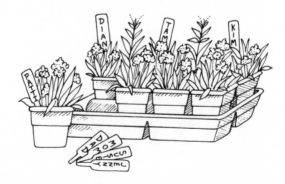

Often a whole flat of flowers, veggies or herbs is more than
you need. Check with family & friends to see if they'd like
to swap. It's fun to pass along plants and create your own
friendship garden.

Farmhouse Sides & Salads

FRESH FARMHOUSE
Recipes

Rosemary's Corn Salad

Rosemary Lightbown
Wakefield, RI

*My daughters always ask for this salad if we are getting together.
It's easy and yummy...makes a great side dish for those summer
days! I sometimes add small mozzarella balls to this salad.*

6 ears corn, cooked and kernels
   removed, or 2 c. frozen corn
2 c. cherry tomatoes, halved
1 c. cucumber, peeled, seeded
   and diced
1/2 c. red onion, diced

6 green onions, thinly sliced
1/4 c. red wine vinegar
1/2 c. olive oil
salt and pepper to taste
1/2 c. fresh basil, chopped

Combine all vegetables in a large bowl; toss to mix and set aside. Add
vinegar to a small bowl. Whisk in olive oil; season with salt and pepper.
Drizzle dressing over salad and toss. Top with chopped basil. Cover and
chill until serving time Makes 6 to 8 servings.

Nothing perks up the flavor of tomatoes like fresh basil!
Keep a pot of basil in the kitchen windowsill and just
pinch off a few leaves whenever they're needed.

Farmhouse
Sides & Salads

Summer Squash Medley

Donna Hamilton
Snyder, TX

This is a great summertime treat! It looks so pretty too. There are times when we just eat a vegetable supper, so we enjoy this dish with some fresh grilled corn on the cob and sliced cucumbers on the side. Delicious!

1 T. butter
1 to 2 yellow squash, diced
1 to 2 zucchini, diced

lemon pepper seasoning and
    salt to taste
14-1/2 oz. can diced tomatoes

Melt butter in a skillet over medium heat. Add squash and zucchini; sauté until tender. Sprinkle with seasonings. Add tomatoes with juice; simmer for 10 minutes, stirring occasionally. Serves 4.

Bok Choy & Mushrooms

Brenda Rogers
Atwood, CA

This is a wonderful vegetable side dish that's quick and tasty. Feel free to use your favorite kind of mushrooms.

1 T. sesame oil
1/4 c. butter
2 c. mushrooms, sliced
    or quartered

1 bunch bok choy, cut into
    1-inch pieces
1 t. garlic powder
salt and pepper to taste

Heat sesame oil in a large skillet over medium-high heat. Add butter and let it melt. Add mushrooms; sauté for several minutes. Add bok choy and stir; add garlic powder and stir. Cook until vegetables are tender, stirring occasionally. Season with salt and pepper. Makes 4 servings.

Fresh air and sunshine are hard to beat.
—Laura Ingalls Wilder

FRESH FARMHOUSE
Recipes

Warm Veggie Side Salad

Vivian Marshall
Columbus, OH

This is a great change from a traditional salad or coleslaw, and it's just delicious. It's a favorite with barbecue chicken and corn on the cob. Leftovers are tasty (if there are any!) and can be enjoyed warmed up as a salad, or to top a burger, hot dog or chicken sandwich.

6 slices bacon
1/2 c. yellow onion, chopped
1/2 c. green pepper, chopped
4 c. cabbage, shredded

2 c. cherry tomatoes, halved
2 to 3 jalapeño peppers, sliced
   and seeded, if desired
1/4 c. chili powder

In a large skillet over medium heat, cook bacon until almost crisp. Remove bacon to paper towels to drain, reserving drippings in pan. Add onion and green pepper to drippings; sauté for about 2 minutes. Add cabbage; cook until soft but not completely limp, stirring often. Add tomatoes, jalapeños and chili powder. Cook and stir for just a few minutes, until heated through but not softened; cabbage and jalapeños should still be crisp. Divide salad among plates or bowls; sprinkle with crumbled bacon and serve. Makes 5 to 6 servings.

Many garden-fresh veggies will stay fresh longer in the refrigerator. Exceptions are potatoes, sweet potatoes, onions and eggplants, which can be kept on the counter. Tomatoes will also keep their sun-ripened flavor best if stored on the windowsill or counter.

Farmhouse Sides & Salads

Mediterranean-Style Potatoes

Shirley Howie
Foxboro, MA

This is a hearty country-style dish that I like to serve with roast chicken. The olives give it a wonderful Mediterranean flavor and I like that it can be made in a single pan!

1/4 c. olive oil
1 lb. new potatoes, peeled and
   halved if large
3/4 c. onion, sliced
1 green pepper, cut into strips

2 cloves garlic, minced
1 t. dried oregano
14-1/2 oz. can diced tomatoes
1/4 c. black olives, halved
salt and pepper to taste

Heat olive oil in a skillet over medium heat; sauté potatoes for 5 minutes. Add onion, green pepper, garlic and oregano. Cook for 5 minutes, or until onion is lightly golden and green pepper has softened. Add tomatoes with juice and bring to a boil; reduce heat to medium-low. Cover and simmer for 25 minutes, stirring occasionally. Add olives during the last 5 minutes of cooking. Season with salt and pepper to taste. Makes 4 servings.

To freshen a wooden cutting board, brush generously with lemon juice and let stand for 30 minutes. Then scrub with a moistened cloth and a little baking soda, rinse and let dry.

FRESH FARMHOUSE
Recipes

Baked Mozzarella Tomatoes

Beth Richter
Canby, MN

This is a favorite of mine. It's best with tomatoes fresh from the garden, but it's so good that I will use tomatoes from the grocery store when I get a craving. I'm also a cheese lover, so I use the full four cups of cheese. I love the convenience of real bacon bits, so sometimes I'll use them too...just as delicious and less mess!

4 to 5 ripe tomatoes, sliced
   and divided
8 c. soft bread cubes
3 to 4 c. shredded mozzarella
   cheese, divided
4 slices bacon, cooked and
   crumbled, or 2.8-oz. pkg.
   real bacon bits

1/2 c. butter, melted
2 eggs, beaten
2 t. onion salt
1/2 t. garlic salt
1/2 t. dried oregano
Optional: 1/2 c. celery, chopped

Arrange half of tomatoes in a greased 13"x9" baking pan in a single layer; set aside. In a large bowl, combine bread cubes, 2 cups cheese, bacon, melted butter, eggs, seasonings and celery, if using. Mix well; spoon over tomatoes. Top with remaining tomatoes; sprinkle with remaining cheese. Bake, uncovered, at 350 degrees for 30 minutes, or until heated through and cheese is melted. Serves 10 to 12.

When chopping veggies, set the cutting board on a damp kitchen towel and it won't slip. Works with mixing bowls when you're stirring up batter too.

Fresh Spinach Salad

Joyce Roebuck
Jacksonville, TX

A fresh salad that's sure to be a hit!

10-oz. pkg. fresh spinach, torn
   into small pieces
6 slices bacon, crisply cooked
   and crumbled

3 eggs, hard-boiled, peeled
   and sliced
3 to 4 green onions or 1 red
   onion, thinly sliced

Make Dressing ahead of time; refrigerate. Toss all ingredients together in a large bowl. Just before serving, add one cup Dressing; toss again. Makes 6 to 8 servings.

Dressing:

1/3 c. oil
1/4 c. vinegar
1/3 c. catsup
1/3 c. sugar

2 T. Worcestershire sauce
1 t. salt
1/2 t. onion powder
1/2 t. garlic powder

Combine all ingredients in a jar; cover and shake well. Keep refrigerated. Makes 2 cups, enough for 2 salads.

When you're on vacation, ask around and find a farmers' market nearby. It's fun to taste locally grown foods that might not be available in your hometown.

FRESH FARMHOUSE
Recipes

Karen's White Bean Salad
Rosemary Lightbown
Wakefield, RI

This recipe is a favorite of mine. A friend shared it years ago, and I have been making it ever since. It's simple and quick to put together. I have made it my own over the years.

15-1/2 oz. can small white
    beans, drained and rinsed
1 red pepper, diced
1/2 c. fresh parsley, chopped

1/4 c. red onion, chopped
1/4 c. fresh chives, chopped
    and divided

Make Dressing; set aside. Combine all ingredients in a large bowl, reserving one tablespoon chives for garnish. Pour dressing over salad; toss to mix and let stand for one hour before serving. Sprinkle with reserved chives. Serves 6.

Dressing:

2 T. lemon juice
2 t. white wine vinegar
1 T. olive oil

1 clove garlic, minced
1/4 t. pepper

In a small bowl, combine lemon juice and vinegar. Whisk in olive oil; stir in garlic and pepper.

Use extra-virgin olive oil for delicately flavored salad dressings and dipping sauces. Less-expensive light olive oil is fine for cooking.

Farmhouse
Sides & Salads

Garden Relish Salad

Delores Lakes
Mansfield, OH

A wonderful summer picnic salad! It is colorful, nutritious and tasty.
You can use cooked fresh green beans, if you like. Use your favorite
bottled Italian dressing, or make your own.

1-1/2 c. cauliflower flowerets
15 cherry tomatoes, halved
1/2 cucumber, sliced
14-1/2 oz. can French-cut green
  beans, drained
Optional: 1/2 c. sliced black
  olives

1/2 t. dill weed
1/2 t. salt
1/2 c. Italian salad dressing
Optional: 1/4 c. crumbled feta
  cheese

Combine vegetables in a large bowl; add olives, if using. Sprinkle with
dill weed and salt; stir in salad dressing. Cover and chill at least 2 hours
before serving. Sprinkle with feta cheese at serving time, if desired.
Makes 6 servings.

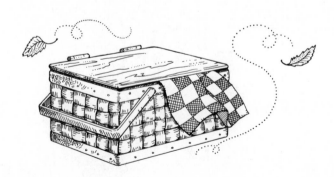

Get ready for spur-of-the-moment picnics on sunny days!
Tuck a basket filled with picnic supplies into the car trunk
along with a quilt to sit on.

FRESH FARMHOUSE
Recipes

Savory Spinach with Cheese *Athena Colegrove*
Big Springs, TX

My family likes spinach, even the kids! This cheesy casserole
is pure comfort in a dish.

2 10-oz. pkgs. frozen chopped
  spinach
2 c. pasteurized process cheese,
  diced
4 eggs, beaten
2/3 c. milk
1/4 c. butter, melted

1/2 c. onion, chopped
2 T. dried parsley
1 t. Worcestershire sauce
1/2 t. dried thyme
1/2 t. nutmeg
1 t. salt

Cook spinach according to package directions; drain well and transfer to
a large bowl. Add cheese; mix well. In a separate bowl, mix remaining
ingredients; add to spinach mixture and stir well. Transfer to a greased
shallow 2-quart casserole dish. Bake, uncovered, at 350 degrees for
40 to 45 minutes, until hot and bubbly. Serves 8.

Substitute fresh baby spinach in any recipe that calls for
frozen spinach. Add one pound fresh spinach and 2 tablespoons
water to a saucepan. Cook over medium-low heat for 3 minutes,
stirring gently until wilted. Then rinse in cold water,
drain and squeeze dry.

Farmhouse Sides & Salads

Grilled Corn & Tomato Salad

JoAnn
Gooseberry Patch

This colorful salad uses all the fresh flavors of a summer garden.

3 ears sweet corn, husks and
   silk removed
1 to 2 ripe tomatoes, cut into
   1/2-inch pieces
2 green onions, thinly sliced

1 orange or yellow pepper,
   cut into 1/2-inch pieces
1 to 2 T. red wine vinegar
1 T. olive oil
salt and pepper to taste

Place corn on a hot, oiled grill over high heat. Cover and cook, turning occasionally, for 8 to 10 minutes, until corn is tender and lightly charred. Cool slightly; cut off kernels using a sharp knife. In a bowl, combine corn and remaining ingredients; toss to mix well. Serve immediately, or cover and chill. Serves 4.

Best Corn Off the Cob

Crystal Shook
Catawba, NC

Just when you think summer sweet corn can't get any better!

6 ears sweet corn, husks
   removed
1/4 c. butter

1/4 c. grated Parmesan cheese
1 t. garlic powder
1 t. Italian seasoning

Add ears of corn to a large pot of boiling water. Boil for 10 to 15 minutes. Remove from heat. Cut corn off the cob into a bowl. Combine remaining ingredients in a microwave-safe bowl. Microwave for one minute, or until butter is melted. Stir and pour over corn; mix well and serve. Makes 4 to 6 servings.

The secret to really sweet, tender corn?
Ideally, you want to pick it, cook it
and enjoy it the same day.

FRESH FARMHOUSE
Recipes

Peppery Mashed Turnips

Courtney Stultz
Weir, KS

After a great turnip season for our garden, we decided to turn one of our favorite sides into a healthier option using the versatile veggie. The results were great...now this is the only way we serve up mashed potatoes!

2 c. turnips, peeled and cut into
   1-inch cubes
1 c. potatoes, peeled and cut
   into 1-inch cubes
3 T. butter
2 T. reduced-fat cream cheese
   or sour cream

1 t. fresh parsley, chopped
1/2 t. garlic powder
1 t. sea salt
1/4 t. pepper
1/8 t. chipotle pepper
1/8 t. chili powder

In a large saucepan, combine turnips and potato. Cover with water and lid. Bring to a boil over medium-high heat. Simmer for about 15 to 20 minutes, until fork-tender. Drain; stir in remaining ingredients. and mash until smooth. Makes 6 servings.

For a real farmhouse feel, make the most of your front porch! Hanging baskets of flowers and a porch swing with comfy pillows create a cozy place for family & friends to visit and enjoy the fresh air.

Farmhouse Sides & Salads

Zesty Lemon Coleslaw

Lynda Hart
Bluffdale, UT

I serve this salad with baked fish and it is so delicious.

1 head green cabbage, cut into
   chunks
1/2 head purple cabbage, cut
   into chunks
1 carrot, peeled
1 red onion, thinly sliced
1 red pepper, diced
1 c. mayonnaise

1 T. honey or sugar
1 t. garlic powder
1/2 t. salt
1/2 t. white pepper or
   lemon pepper
zest of 1 lemon
1/2 c. lemon juice, or to taste

Finely grate cabbages and carrot in a food processor; transfer to a large bowl. Add onion and red pepper; set aside. In another bowl, whisk together remaining ingredients into a thin smooth sauce, adding lemon juice to taste. Add dressing to cabbage mixture and toss well. Cover and chill at least one hour before serving. Serves 6.

A rustic watering can makes a charming centerpiece filled with stems of cutting-garden favorites like Chinese lanterns, silver dollar plant and bells of Ireland.

FRESH FARMHOUSE
Recipes

Garden-Fresh Potato Salad

*JoAnn
Gooseberry Patch*

*Fresh green beans and zesty red pepper make this
potato salad anything but ordinary!*

1-1/2 lbs. new potatoes, cubed
3/4 lb. fresh green beans, cut
    into 1-1/2 inch pieces
1 red pepper, chopped
1 red onion, chopped
1/4 c. olive oil

1/4 c. cider vinegar
2 T. Dijon mustard
1 t. fresh parsley, chopped
1 t. fresh dill, chopped
1 t. sugar
1/2 t. salt

In a large saucepan, cover potatoes with water. Bring to a boil over
high heat; boil for 10 minutes. Add green beans; boil an additional
10 minutes, or until potatoes are fork-tender. Drain; let cool and transfer
to a large serving bowl. Add red pepper and onion; set aside. Whisk
together remaining ingredients in a small bowl. Pour over vegetables;
toss until well coated. Cover and chill thoroughly before serving.
Serves 8 to 10.

For a fresh change from spinach, give Swiss chard a try.
An old-time favorite, it's easy to serve too...just steam until
tender and drizzle with cider vinegar to taste.

Farmhouse Sides & Salads

Sheet Pan Spiralizer Potatoes

Jenita Davison
La Plata, MO

I love new kitchen gadgets! My spiralizer is fun to play with and makes this potato recipe healthier than fries. It can be seasoned however you like, but this is our favorite. Sometimes I mix in some chopped onion, too.

2 large russet potatoes, peeled
2 t. canola oil
1 t. garlic powder
1 t. chili powder

1 t. paprika
1 t. ground cumin
1 t. salt
1 t. pepper

Cut potatoes with a spiralizer, using a thick spiral blade. Place on a silicone-lined baking sheet. Drizzle lightly with oil, tossing to coat. Sprinkle with seasonings; mix again. Bake at 450 degrees for about 20 to 25 minutes. Place pan under the broiler for just a few minutes, until potatoes are crisp. Serve hot. Makes 4 servings.

Fresh herbs give a wonderful flavor boost to vegetable dishes!
If a recipe calls for one teaspoon of a dried herb, simply
substitute one tablespoon of the fresh herb.

FRESH FARMHOUSE
Recipes

Cauliflower Tater Salad

Susan Jacobs
Vista, CA

For years, I've been cutting carbs and altering my old favorites, so I decided to switch up my usual potato salad. I was surprised at how much my hubby liked it!

2 lbs. cauliflower, cut into
   small flowerets
5 eggs, hard-boiled and peeled
1/2 c. celery, diced
1/2 c. dill pickle relish
1 T. mustard

1 to 1-1/2 c. mayonnaise
salt and pepper to taste
paprika to taste
Optional: chopped green onions,
   sliced black olives

Spread cauliflower evenly on a parchment paper-lined baking sheet. Bake at 375 degrees for about 16 minutes, just until tender. Remove from oven and let cool. Grate eggs using a cheese grater, or chop with a knife. Combine cooled cauliflower and eggs in a large bowl; add celery, relish and mustard. Stir in one cup mayonnaise; add more as needed. Gently stir until well combined; season with salt and pepper. Transfer salad to a serving bowl. Lightly sprinkle with paprika; garnish with onions and olives, if desired. Keep refrigerated. Serves 6 to 8.

Frame cherished handwritten recipes to hang in the kitchen. They'll bring back sweet memories and will always be nearby when you want to prepare them.

Farmhouse Sides & Salads

Homecoming Broccoli Salad

Eileen Bennett
Jenison, MI

Traveling within a radius of 60 miles, ten of us ladies met every December for many years to renew our friendships and share good food. This salad became a tradition in 1982. My family loves it too.

2 bunches broccoli, cut into
   bite-size flowerets
2 lbs. sliced mushrooms

4 green onions, including a bit
   of the tops, sliced

Mix vegetables together in a large bowl. Pour Dressing over top; toss to mix well. Cover and refrigerate 2 hours before serving. Makes 6 to 8 servings.

Dressing:

1 c. salad or olive oil
1/4 c. white vinegar
1/2 c. sugar
1 t. paprika

1 t. celery seed
1 t. salt
Optional: 1 t. onion powder

Combine all ingredients in a bowl. Beat with an electric mixer on low speed until well blended.

The next time you see a roadside stand in the country, stop and take a look! You're sure to find the freshest fruits & veggies, cut flowers and even homemade goodies like pickles, preserves, pies and cakes.

FRESH FARMHOUSE
Recipes

Mason Jar Cucumber Salad

Tracy Meyers
Alexandria, KY

This is a favorite with my family. And even better, it's super easy!

7 c. pickling cucumbers,
    thinly sliced
1 c. white onion, thinly sliced
1/2 c. red, orange or yellow
    pepper, sliced
1/2 c. green pepper, sliced
1 T. salt

1-1/2 c. white vinegar
2 c. sugar
1 t. celery seed
1-1/2 t. mustard seed
2 1-qt. canning jars with lids,
    sterilized

In a large bowl, combine cucumbers, onion and peppers. Sprinkle with salt; stir well and set aside for one hour. Meanwhile, in a saucepan, mix vinegar, sugar, celery seed and mustard seed. Stir and bring to a boil. Remove from heat; set aside for one hour. Divide vegetables evenly between 2 quart-size canning jars; ladle cooled vinegar mixture over vegetables. Cover jars with lids; refrigerate overnight before serving. Makes 2 quarts.

For the tastiest, healthiest meals, choose from a rainbow of veggies...red beets, orange sweet potatoes, yellow summer squash, dark green kale and Brussels sprouts, purple eggplant and blueberries. Fill your plate and eat up!

Farmhouse Sides & Salads

Marinated Tomatoes

Barb Bargdill
Gooseberry Patch

*A fresh and flavorful way to enjoy a variety of heirloom
tomatoes from the farmers' market.*

2 lbs. assorted ripe tomatoes,
   coarsely chopped
1 shallot, minced
1/2 c. red wine vinegar
3 T. olive oil

3 cloves garlic, pressed
1-1/2 t. sea salt
1/2 t. pepper
1 c. fresh basil, chopped
1/4 c. fresh parsley, chopped

In a large bowl, combine tomatoes and shallot. In another bowl, whisk
together remaining ingredients except herbs; pour over tomato mixture.
Toss gently to mix. Let stand for one hour and 45 minutes, tossing
occasionally. Stir in basil and parsley just before serving. Makes about
4 cups.

Marinated Green Bean Salad

Judy Phelan
Macomb, IL

*This is an excellent vegetable salad, served chilled. I have it
on a well-worn recipe card from my mother's recipe box.*

15-1/2 oz. can dark red kidney
   beans, drained
14-1/2 oz. can cut green beans,
   drained
14-1/2 oz. can wax beans,
   drained
1/2 c. green pepper, diced

1/2 c. onion, chopped
3/4 c. sugar
1/2 c. oil
1/2 c. vinegar
1 t. salt
1/2 t. pepper

In a large bowl, combine all beans. Add remaining ingredients; mix well.
Cover and refrigerate for 4 to 5 hours before serving. Serves 8.

FRESH FARMHOUSE
Recipes

Wendy's Harvest Salad

Wendy Lee Paffenroth
Pine Island, NY

Shortly after my husband and I were married, we inherited a backyard orchard. Soon we purchased the surrounding property and before long, we had 400 apple trees of all varieties. Everyone started giving me apple recipes! I started coming up with my own as well. This salad made with our own apples was always a hit at potlucks and family gatherings.

1-1/2 c. red Empire or Cortland
   apples, cored and diced
1 c. celery, diced
1/2 to 3/4 c. chopped walnuts
   or pecans
1 c. red seedless grapes
1 c. raisins

3/4 c. mayonnaise
1/4 c. sour cream
1 t. sugar
salt to taste
1/8 t. fresh chives, chopped
Optional: lettuce leaves

In a large bowl, combine apples, celery, nuts, grapes and raisins; set aside. In a separate bowl, whisk together remaining ingredients except optional lettuce. Pour over apple mixture; mix gently until well coated. Cover and chill until serving time. Serve cold, spooned into a bowl lined with lettuce leaves if desired. Makes 6 servings.

Keep chopped apples from turning brown while you prepare other ingredients. Combine one cup of water and one tablespoon lemon juice. Add apples and soak for several minutes, then drain and rinse.

Farmhouse Sides & Salads

Creamy Cucumber Salad

Evangeline Boston
Bradley Junction, FL

A delicious cool salad for summer! I found this easy recipe few years back in an old cookbook and adjusted it to fit my taste.

3 to 5 cucumbers, peeled, halved
    lengthwise and seeded
1/2 c. red onion, thinly sliced
2 to 3 T. cider vinegar

1/2 c. sour cream
1/4 c. fresh dill, snipped
1 t. sugar, or more to taste
salt and pepper to taste

On a large plate, drain cucumber halves cut-side down on paper towels. Refrigerate for 20 minutes; slice thinly. Meanwhile, combine onion and vinegar in a bowl; set aside for 15 minutes. In a serving bowl, mix together sour cream, dill, sugar, salt and pepper. Add cucumbers and onion mixture; toss gently. Cover and chill before serving. Serves 4 to 6.

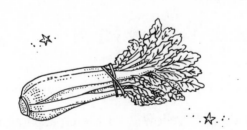

Don't toss out the leaves from fresh celery...they're full
of flavor! Lay them on a paper towel, and allow to dry for
a day or two. Store the dried leaves in a canning jar to
toss into soups, stews and casseroles.

FRESH FARMHOUSE
Recipes

Parmesan Green Beans & Lemon Casserole

Annette Ceravolo
Birmingham, AL

A scrumptious, fresh change from green beans with mushroom soup.

8 c. water
1 T. plus 1 t. salt, divided
2 lbs. fresh green beans, trimmed
2 T. butter
1/3 c. all-purpose flour

4 c. milk
1 c. grated Parmesan cheese
1 T. lemon zest
1 c. panko bread crumbs

In a saucepan over high heat, bring water and one tablespoon salt to a boil. Add beans and cook for 4 to 5 minutes, until tender; drain. Melt butter in a separate saucepan over medium heat. Add flour, whisking constantly. Gradually add milk, stirring constantly until smooth. Add cheese, zest and remaining salt. Stir in green beans; mix well. Transfer to a 13"x9" baking pan sprayed with non-stick vegetable spray. Sprinkle with bread crumbs. Bake, uncovered, at 400 degrees for about 15 to 20 minutes, until golden. Serves 6 to 8.

Asparagus & Yellow Rice

Jo Ann Belovitch
Stratford, CT

A quick & easy dish to serve with your favorite roast.

7-oz. pkg. Spanish-style yellow
   rice, uncooked
2 to 3 cubes chicken bouillon
2 T. olive oil or butter

1 bunch asparagus, trimmed
   and chopped
Optional: salt and pepper to taste

Prepare rice according to package directions, adding bouillon cubes and oil or butter to cooking water. Add asparagus during the last 10 minutes of cooking time; season with salt and pepper, if desired. Makes 6 servings.

Remove beet stains from your hands by sprinkling hands
with baking soda and a little water. Scrub well, rinse and
repeat as necessary.

Farmhouse Sides & Salads

Mom's Favorite Zucchini Casserole

Marsha Baker
Pioneer, OH

My mom sure loved this dish! Once she made it for a progressive dinner for teens from church. After she made it, she was concerned they might not like it. She giggled when she told me they'd cleaned up her dish! This can also be turned into a one-dish meal by adding some chopped cooked chicken.

4 c. zucchini, peeled and diced
salt to taste
1 carrot, peeled and grated
1 onion, grated
10-3/4 oz. can cream of
   chicken soup
1 c. sour cream
6-oz. pkg. chicken-flavored
   stuffing mix
salt and pepper to taste
1 c. corn flake cereal, crushed
1/4 c. butter, melted

Cook zucchini in a large saucepan of salted boiling water for 4 minutes; drain. In a large bowl, combine zucchini and remaining ingredients except cereal and butter. Mix well and spread in a greased 9"x9" baking pan. Toss cereal with melted butter; sprinkle over top. Bake, uncovered, at 350 degrees for 45 minutes, or until bubbly and golden. Makes 6 to 8 servings.

Steam vegetables to keep their fresh-picked taste. Bring 1/2 inch water to a boil in a saucepan; add cut-up veggies. Cover and cook about 3 to 5 minutes, to desired tenderness. Toss with a little butter or olive oil...ready to serve.

FRESH FARMHOUSE
Recipes

Gruyère Potato Gratin

Vickie
Gooseberry Patch

*In this rich and creamy recipe, scalloped potatoes are
at their very best. Just wait for the oohs and aahs!*

2 lbs. Yukon Gold potatoes,
  peeled, sliced and divided
6-oz. pkg. Gruyère cheese,
  coarsely shredded and
  divided
salt and pepper to taste

1 c. milk
1 c. whipping cream
nutmeg to taste
Garnish: thinly sliced green
  onions

Cook potatoes in a large saucepan of boiling water for 4 minutes; drain.
Layer 1/3 of potato slices in a greased 3-quart casserole dish; sprinkle
with 1/2 cup cheese, salt and pepper to taste. Repeat layering; top with
remaining potato slices. Set aside. Combine milk and cream in a heavy
saucepan over medium-low heat; heat just to boiling. Whisk in nutmeg;
spoon over potatoes. Sprinkle remaining cheese on top. Bake, uncovered,
at 400 degrees for 30 minutes, or until golden and potatoes are tender.
Garnish with green onions. Makes 4 to 6 servings.

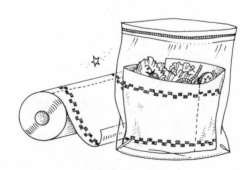

Keep salad greens farmstand-fresh up to a week. Rinse in
cool water, wrap in paper towels and slip into a plastic zipping
bag with several small holes cut in it. Tuck the bag in the
fridge's crisper bin....ready to serve when you are!

Farmhouse Sides & Salads

Deviled Green Beans

Joan Baker
Westland, MI

*I received this recipe from my sister-in-law Diane. It is
a nice change of pace from plain green beans.*

1/2 lb. fresh green beans,
   trimmed
1-1/2 t. butter

1 t. mustard
1/2 t. Worcestershire sauce
salt and pepper to taste

Cook beans in a large saucepan of boiling water for 3 minutes, or until
tender. Drain; transfer to a serving dish. Melt butter in a small saucepan
over low heat; stir in remaining ingredients. Pour over beans; stir gently
and serve. Makes 4 servings.

Easy Roasted Brussels Sprouts

Shirley Howie
Foxboro, MA

*This side dish is so easy to put together, as you don't need to precook
the bacon. It bakes right along with the sprouts! Parmesan cheese
adds another layer of wonderful flavor to this delicious recipe.*

1 lb. fresh Brussels sprouts,
   trimmed and quartered
4 slices thick-cut bacon,
   chopped

2 T. olive oil
2 cloves garlic, minced
salt and pepper to taste
1/4 c. grated Parmesan cheese

In a bowl, combine Brussels sprouts, bacon, olive oil, garlic, salt and
pepper; stir until well mixed. Spread mixture evenly on a greased baking
sheet. Bake at 400 degrees for 20 to 25 minutes, until sprouts are
tender and golden. Transfer to a serving dish. Sprinkle with Parmesan
cheese, tossing to coat. Serves 4 to 5.

Shopping at a farmstand? Keep
fruits & veggies farm-fresh by
packing them in a cooler in
your car.

FRESH FARMHOUSE
Recipes

Marinated Veggie Salad

Cindy Mitchell
Maroa, IL

I keep a container of this salad marinating in the fridge all summer because my husband loves it so much! I use fresh vegetables as well as basil whenever I can find them at a farmers' market.

2 to 3 ripe tomatoes, sliced
1 small onion, halved and sliced

1 cucumber, peeled, halved
 and sliced

Combine all vegetables in a large bowl. Pour Dressing over vegetables; dressing should just cover vegetables. Cover and refrigerate at least one hour before serving. Serve with a slotted spoon. Serves 6.

Dressing:

1 c. canola or olive oil
6 T. white vinegar
2 T. sugar or powdered
 sweetener
2 t. Worcestershire sauce

4 t. fresh basil, chopped,
 or 2 t. dried basil
1/4 t. pepper
1/8 t. dried thyme

Whisk together all ingredients.

Garden-fresh vegetables are delicious steamed and topped with pats of chive butter. Blend 1/4 cup softened butter with 2 tablespoons chopped fresh chives, one teaspoon lemon zest and a little salt & pepper...yum!

Farmhouse Sides & Salads

Summer Garden Vegetable Medley

Beverly Jones
Bernice, LA

My sister-in-law shared this recipe many years ago and it is one of our favorite side dishes featuring summer veggies. Enjoy with fresh sliced tomatoes.

1 c. potatoes, peeled and diced
1 c. yellow squash, diced
1 c. zucchini, diced
1 c. okra, sliced

1/2 c. onion, diced
salt and pepper to taste
1 c. yellow cornmeal
oil for frying

In a large bowl, mix all vegetables together. Season with salt and pepper; sprinkle with cornmeal and mix well until vegetables are coated. Heat several inches oil in a skillet over medium-high heat. Carefully add about 1-1/2 cups vegetable mixture to oil. Cook until tender and lightly golden; drain on paper towels. Repeat with remaining vegetables; serve warm. Serves 4 to 6.

A child on a farm sees a plane fly overhead and dreams of a faraway place. A traveler on the plane sees the farmhouse...and dreams of home.

–Carl Burns

FRESH FARMHOUSE
Recipes

Angel Hair Pasta Salad

Barbara Klein
Newburgh, IN

*My sister-in-law Michele gave me this recipe and it has become
a family favorite. I often take this to carry-in dinners and everyone
loves it! The flavors mingle as it chills and it's just delicious.*

16-oz. pkg. angel hair pasta,
  uncooked
1/4 c. plus 1 T. oil
1/4 c. lemon juice
2-1/2 T. seasoned salt, or to taste
1-1/4 c. celery, sliced

2/3 c. green pepper, chopped
3/4 c. yellow onion, green onions
  or shallots, chopped
3/4 c. black olives, chopped
1 to 2 ripe tomatoes, diced
1-1/2 c. mayonnaise

Cook pasta according to package directions; drain. Rinse with cool
water; drain and transfer to a large bowl. In a small bowl, mix together
oil, lemon juice and salt; add to pasta and toss gently. Cover and
refrigerate for 8 to 10 hours. Add remaining ingredients; mix well and
chill until serving time. Serves 10 to 12.

No more trying to keep tomato plants upright in the garden!
Plant pint-size cherry tomato plants in hanging baskets filled
with potting soil. They'll grow beautifully...upside-down!

Farmhouse Sides & Salads

Christy's Broccoli-Bacon Salad
Georgia Muth
Penn Valley, CA

I grew up on the central coast of California, where the fertile soil yields acres and acres of broccoli. Because it's so plentiful, we use broccoli in many recipes. This fresh salad recipe is made often by my dear friend, Christy.

1/2 lb. bacon, crisply cooked and chopped
1-1/2 lbs. broccoli, finely chopped

1/2 c. purple onion, sliced or diced
1 c. sweetened dried cranberries
1 c. chopped cashews or peanuts

Combine all ingredients in a large bowl. Add Dressing; mix until well coated. Cover and chill until serving time. Serves 6 to 8.

Dressing:

1 c. mayonnaise
1/4 c. sugar

1 T. red wine vinegar

Combine all ingredients; mix well.

For hearty salads in a snap, keep cans of black olives, garbanzo beans and marinated artichokes in the fridge. They'll be chilled and ready to toss with fresh greens and juicy tomatoes at a moment's notice.

FRESH FARMHOUSE
Recipes

Summer Squash Salad

Gladys Kielar
Whitehouse, OH

*Every year, we have plenty of summer squash from our garden,
so we make this refreshing salad to share with family & friends.*

4 c. yellow squash, sliced into
   very thin strips
4 c. zucchini, sliced into very
   thin strips
2 c. radishes, sliced
2 c. canola oil

1/3 c. cider vinegar
2 T. Dijon mustard
2 T. fresh parsley, snipped
1 t. dried dill weed
1-1/2 t. salt
1/2 t. pepper

In a large bowl, toss together yellow squash, zucchini and radishes; set
aside. In a jar with a tight-fitting lid, combine remaining ingredients;
shake well and pour over squash mixture. Cover and refrigerate for at
least 2 hours. Serves 10 to 12.

Try your hand at vegetable gardening! Even the smallest yard
is sure to have a sunny corner where you can grow sun-ripened
tomatoes and an herb plant or two. Seeds, plants and
free advice are available at the nearest garden store.

Farmhouse Sides & Salads

Country Greens & New Potatoes
Jill Valentine
Jackson, TN

A tasty old-fashioned way to serve fresh garden greens.

1 bunch Swiss chard, spinach,
   kale or collard greens, rinsed
   and stems removed
1/4 lb. lean salt pork, sliced

4 to 6 potatoes, quartered
cider vinegar, butter, salt and
   pepper to taste

Add greens to a large soup pot, pressing down as needed. Top with salt pork. Cook over medium-low to medium heat for 20 minutes, stirring occasionally. Add potatoes and enough water to cover potatoes. Cook another 25 to 30 minutes, until potatoes, greens and pork are tender. Drain. Serve greens and potatoes seasoned as desired with vinegar, butter, salt and pepper. Serve pork alongside greens, if desired. Serves 4.

Sheet Pan Roasted Beets
Patty Flak
Erie, PA

If you think you don't like beets, just give these a try!

2 lbs. beets, peeled and cut into
   1/2-inch cubes
1 large onion, halved and sliced
2 T. balsamic vinegar

1 T. olive oil
1/2 t. coarse salt
1/2 t. pepper

In a large bowl, toss vegetables with remaining ingredients. Spread in a single layer on a 15"x10" jelly-roll pan. Bake at 400 degrees for 45 minutes, stirring several times, until beets are tender. Serves 4.

To keep rice from getting sticky, don't stir it after cooking.
Instead, gently fluff it with a fork. Works every time!

FRESH FARMHOUSE
Recipes

Farmers' Market Corn Toss

Dale Duncan
Waterloo, IA

This is a delicious side dish to serve with grilled or roasted chicken and pork...perfect for picnics! For a yummy meatless main, combine it with mini bowtie pasta.

1 T. olive oil
1/2 c. sweet onion, diced
1 red pepper, diced
2 ears sweet corn, kernels
    removed
2 zucchini, thinly sliced

1/4 c. fresh parsley, chopped
garlic powder to taste
1/4 t. salt
1/4 t. pepper
1/4 c. grated Parmesan cheese,
    divided

Heat oil in a large skillet on medium heat. Add onion and red pepper; cook and stir for 3 minutes. Stir in corn and zucchini; cook and stir for 5 minutes, or until all vegetables are crisp-tender. Remove from heat. Stir in parsley, seasonings and 2 tablespoons cheese. Top with remaining cheese and serve. Serves 6.

When cutting the kernels from ears of sweet corn, stand the ear in the center of a tube cake pan. The kernels will fall neatly into the pan.

Farmhouse Sides & Salads

Creamy Asparagus Bake

Bethi Hendrickson
Danville, PA

This dish is a spring favorite...it's wonderful for brunch or dinner!

1 lb. asparagus spears, trimmed
2 T. butter
2 T. all-purpose flour
1 c. milk
1 t. lemon juice

salt to taste
3-oz. pkg. cream cheese,
  softened
1/2 c. soft bread crumbs
Optional: nutmeg to taste

Fill a large skillet with 3/4 inch water; bring to a boil over high heat. Add asparagus in a single layer. Cover and cook for 2 to 3 minutes, until tender; drain. Meanwhile, melt butter in a saucepan over medium heat. Blend in flour, milk, lemon juice and salt until thickened. Blend in cream cheese; remove from heat. Arrange asparagus in a buttered 2-quart casserole dish; spoon sauce over top. Sprinkle with bread crumbs. Bake, uncovered, at 350 degrees for 30 minutes. Broil for just a few minutes, until crumbs are golden. Sprinkle with nutmeg, if desired. Serves 6 to 8.

Buttermilk Coleslaw

Beth Flack
Terre Haute, IN

*My grandmother used to make this wonderful coleslaw
for picnics, to serve alongside fried chicken.*

2 c. mayonnaise
1 c. buttermilk
3 T. sugar
1 t. celery seed

1/2 t. pepper
2 16-oz. pkgs. shredded
  coleslaw mix

In a large bowl, stir together mayonnaise, buttermilk, sugar, celery seed and pepper. Fold in coleslaw mix until well coated. Cover and refrigerate at least 3 hours before serving. Serves 8 to 10.

Shredding your own cabbage? You'll need about 7 cups shredded cabbage to equal a 16-ounce package.

FRESH FARMHOUSE
Recipes

Mama's Grillin' Corn

Kassie Frazier
Westpoint, TN

At our house, I am the Queen of the Grill! I love to grill and my husband and kids love to eat my grilled goodies. One of my favorite vegetables to grill is corn on the cob. We like Peaches & Cream sweet corn. Every summer I go to purchase fresh corn and other fresh vegetables and fruit from the Amish in our community. Enjoy some of the best corn you will ever eat!

6 ears sweet corn on the cob
   in husks
1/2 c. butter, softened

1 T. sea salt
1 T. pepper

Peel back husks of corn; remove silk. Brush corn with butter; lightly season with salt and pepper; pull the husks back up. Wrap each ear in aluminum foil. Grill over medium heat for 10 minutes, turning once. Remove from grill. Remove the foil from each ear; pull off husks and serve. Makes 6 servings.

Dad's Asparagus

Ann Farris
Biscoe, AR

Many years ago, my dad started an asparagus bed that we still enjoy today. Special memories on the farm! Simple and oh-so good.

4 to 6 slices bacon, chopped
1 lb. asparagus, ends trimmed

salt and pepper to taste

Cook bacon in a skillet over medium heat until crisp. Remove bacon to a paper towel, reserving drippings in pan. Add asparagus to drippings. Cook for 8 to 10 minutes, tossing often. Season with salt and pepper; toss with crumbled bacon and serve. Serves 6.

Serve up salad dressings in old-fashioned pint milk bottles...charming!

106

Farmhouse Sides & Salads

Cranberry-Almond Salad

Marla Kinnersley
Surprise, AZ

Whenever I bring this salad to a get-together, I always bring home an empty bowl...it's fantastic! It's easy and feeds a crowd...people cannot seem to get enough of it. Great for the holidays, but too good not to serve the rest of the year. I hope you enjoy this salad as much as we have!

1 lb. bacon, crisply cooked
   and crumbled
29-oz. can mandarin oranges,
   drained
12-oz. pkg. sweetened dried
   cranberries

1 lb. baby spinach
2 5-oz. containers crumbled
   feta cheese
3-1/2 oz. pkg. sliced almonds
1/2 c. red onion, thinly sliced
12-oz. bottle poppy seed dressing

In a very large bowl, combine all ingredients except dressing; toss to mix. Cover and chill until serving time. Just before serving, add dressing and toss to coat well. Makes 8 to 10 servings.

It's easy to tote a salad to a picnic. Mix it up in a plastic zipping bag, seal and set it right in the cooler. When you arrive at the picnic grounds, simply tip the salad into a serving bowl.

FRESH FARMHOUSE
Recipes

Grilled Vegetable Pasta Salad

Doreen Knapp
Stanfordville, NY

I always have so many vegetables from my garden that I was trying to think of a great-tasting way to use all of my bounty. My friend told me this was the best salad she'd ever tasted! It's great as a meal, not just a side dish. It's delicious year 'round. Add whatever you like and really make it your own!

16-oz. pkg. bowtie or ziti
   pasta, uncooked
2 T. olive oil, divided
1 zucchini, cut lengthwise
   in thirds
1 yellow squash, cut lengthwise
   in thirds
1 red pepper, quartered
1 red onion, halved

1 bunch fresh asparagus,
   trimmed
1/2 t. Italian seasoning
7-oz. can black olives, drained
   and halved
16-oz. bottle Italian salad
   dressing, divided
Garnish: shaved Parmesan
   cheese

Cook pasta according to package directions; drain. Rinse with cold water; drain again and transfer to a large bowl. Toss pasta with one tablespoon olive oil and set aside. In another large bowl, combine zucchini, squash, red pepper, onion and asparagus. Add remaining oil and Italian seasoning; toss well. Using tongs, arrange all vegetables on a heated grill. Cook about 3 minutes, or until grill marks form. Flip vegetables; cook until fork-tender. Cut into one-inch pieces; add to cooked pasta. Add olives and half of salad dressing; toss well. Top with Parmesan cheese. Serve at room temperature or chilled; add more dressing, if needed. Makes 8 to 10 servings.

Scoop servings of pasta salad into hollowed-out
tomato halves...so pretty on the dining table!

Farmhouse Sides & Salads

Summer Squash Stir-Fry

Ramona Wysong
Barlow, KY

I love fresh vegetables! In the summertime, this is one of my favorite combinations when you have fresh-from-the-garden produce. Some other good seasonings include Creole seasoning, lemon pepper or a pinch or two of oregano.

2 T. olive oil
2 cloves garlic, minced
2 zucchini squash, sliced
2 yellow squash, sliced
2 sweet onions, thinly sliced

2 ripe tomatoes, chopped
salt and pepper to taste
Optional: other seasonings
   to taste

Heat oil in a large skillet or wok over medium heat. Add garlic; cook and stir for about 30 seconds. Add remaining ingredients. Cook over medium heat, stirring occasionally, for about 15 to 20 minutes, until tender. Add seasonings to taste. Serves 3 to 4.

Spread savory herb butter over grilled corn or stir it into whipped potatoes...yum! To make your own, combine 1/2 pound softened butter with 2 pressed garlic cloves, 1/2 teaspoon lemon juice and one tablespoon each chopped fresh parsley and chives or dill.

FRESH FARMHOUSE
Recipes

Old Settlers' Beans

Leona Krivda
Belle Vernon, PA

This is a great old-fashioned recipe I make for picnics and family get-togethers. Everyone has always loved it and the guys like the variety of meats in it.

1/4 lb. bacon
1/2 lb. ground beef
1/4 c. onion, finely diced
14-oz. pkg. Kielbasa sausage,
    sliced in 1/2-inch pieces
15-3/4 oz. can pork & beans
15-1/2 oz. can kidney beans

15-1/2 oz. can butter beans
1/2 c. brown sugar, packed
1/2 c. sugar
1/4 c. catsup
2 T. molasses
1/2 t. mustard

Cook bacon in a skillet over medium heat until crisp. Drain bacon on paper towels; crumble. In the same skillet, cook beef with onion until beef is browned and onion is soft; drain. Combine crumbled bacon, beef mixture and remaining ingredients in a lightly greased 2-quart casserole dish. Cover and bake at 350 degrees for 1-1/2 hours, or until hot and bubbly. Serves 8 to 10.

Spend the day at an auction in the country. Take along a notepad & pencil, a sack lunch and most of all, your imagination! Look for cast-offs that can be put to new use…you never know what you'll find.

Family Dinner Favorites

FRESH FARMHOUSE
Recipes

Zesty Chicken & Broccoli

Courtney Stultz
Weir, KS

This is a great light and refreshing dish featuring fresh vegetables.

2 boneless, skinless chicken
    breasts, cut into chunks
1 T. olive oil
1/2 lb. mushrooms, diced
2 c. broccoli, cut into bite-size
    flowerets

2 c. spinach, chopped
1 c. cherry tomatoes, halved
1 t. garlic, minced
3 T. zesty Italian salad dressing
1 t. sea salt
1/2 t. pepper

In a large skillet over medium heat, sauté chicken in olive oil for about 10 minutes, turning once. Add mushrooms, broccoli, spinach, tomatoes and garlic. Drizzle with dressing; season with salt and pepper. Cook over medium heat for 15 minutes, or until chicken is cooked through. Serves 4.

Make a double batch of your favorite comfort food and invite neighbors over for supper...what a great way to get to know them better. Keep it simple with a tossed salad, warm bakery bread and apple crisp for dessert. It's all about food and fellowship!

Family Dinner Favorites

Garden Goulash

Mary Davis
Rochester, NY

This recipe came about from an overflow of garden veggies.
Feel free to use whatever you have in your own garden!

8-oz. pkg. elbow macaroni, uncooked	3 c. ripe tomatoes, chopped
1 lb. ground beef	2 c. zucchini, chopped
1-1/2 c. onion, chopped	2 c. yellow squash, chopped
1-1/2 c. green pepper, chopped	1 c. mushrooms, chopped
	salt and pepper to taste

Cook macaroni according to package directions; drain. Meanwhile, in a large skillet over medium heat, brown beef with onion and green pepper; drain. Stir in remaining vegetables; cover and simmer for 10 minutes. Season with salt and pepper; serve mixture over cooked macaroni. Makes 4 servings.

Macaroni & Cheese with Tomatoes

Joyce Borrill
Utica, NY

Just a little twist to our favorite mac & cheese. The tomatoes make a nice change! A mix of Cheddar and Swiss cheese can be used.

2 c. cooked elbow macaroni	2 T. butter, sliced
28-oz. can diced tomatoes	salt and pepper to taste
1-1/2 t. onion, minced	
8-oz. pkg. shredded Cheddar cheese, divided	

In a greased 2-quart casserole dish, combine cooked macaroni, tomatoes with juice, onion and 1-1/2 cups cheese; mix well. Dot with pats of butter; season with salt and pepper. Bake, uncovered, at 350 degrees for 45 minutes. Uncover; sprinkle with remaining cheese. Bake 15 minutes longer. Makes 4 to 6 servings.

We all have hometown appetites.
—Clementine Paddleford

FRESH FARMHOUSE
Recipes

Cheesy Country Chicken Casserole

Nancy Lanning
Lancaster, SC

This dish has become a favorite of ours...real comfort food!

1-1/2 c. elbow macaroni, uncooked
10-3/4 oz. can cream of chicken soup
1/3 c. milk
1/4 c. mayonnaise
1/2 t. dry mustard
1/4 t. pepper
2 c. cooked chicken, diced
8-oz. pkg. shredded mozzarella cheese, divided
1 c. buttery round crackers, finely crumbled
2 T. butter, melted

Cook macaroni according to package directions; drain. Meanwhile, stir together soup, milk, mayonnaise and seasonings in a large bowl. Add cooked macaroni, chicken and one cup cheese; mix gently. Transfer to a greased 3-quart casserole dish. Add remaining cheese on top. Combine cracker crumbs and melted butter; sprinkle on top. Bake, uncovered, at 350 degrees for 30 to 40 minutes, until bubbly and cheese is melted. Makes 4 servings.

When the weather is nice, carry dinner to the backyard for a picnic. You'll be making memories together...and just about everything seems to taste even better outdoors!

Family Dinner Favorites

Italian Zucchini Bake

Cyndi Chapman
Brackney, PA

One summer, my husband and I had stopped eating pasta but were craving Italian food. All the farmers' markets were full of fresh vegetables, so I made up this Italian dish...it really satisfied our craving!

1-1/2 lbs. ground spicy or
   mild pork sausage
8-oz. can tomato sauce
3 cloves garlic, minced
1 t. dried tarragon
1 t. salt
1/4 t. pepper
2 medium zucchini, sliced
   1/4-inch thick and divided

2 medium yellow squash, sliced
   1/4-inch thick and divided
2 ripe tomatoes, thinly sliced
   and divided
1 onion, thinly sliced and divided
8-oz. pkg. shredded mozzarella
   cheese, divided

Brown sausage in a skillet over medium heat; drain. Add tomato sauce, garlic and seasonings; cook and stir until well blended. Spread 1/3 of sausage mixture in a greased 13"x9" baking pan. Layer with 1/3 each of zucchini, squash, tomatoes, onion and cheese. Repeat layering twice, but do not add remaining 1/3 of cheese. Bake, uncovered, at 375 degrees for 60 minutes. Sprinkle remaining cheese on top; broil for another 10 minutes. Remove from oven; let stand for 15 minutes before serving. To serve, ladle into shallow bowls. Serves 8.

Try using a little less ground beef in your favorite recipe.
Add a few more chopped veggies...there's a good chance
that no one will even notice!

FRESH FARMHOUSE
Recipes

Angel Hair with Zucchini & Tomatoes

Marcia Shaffer
Conneaut Lake, PA

One summer, I had more zucchini than I knew what to do with, tomatoes in abundance and the neighbors all well satisfied with handouts. The grandkids were coming back from the lake, hungry as bears and wanting to be fed quickly. I just put together what I had the most of, in my biggest pot, and served it with pasta. The grandkids said, "Grandma, why haven't you made this for us before?" Surprise, they loved it and now request often it in the hot summer days! Healthy too. Sometimes those toss-together recipes turn out better than you expected!

8-oz. pkg. angel hair pasta,
   uncooked
4 t. extra-virgin olive oil
4 cloves garlic, chopped
2 shallots, diced
2 zucchini, cut lengthwise
   into thin ribbons
salt and pepper to taste

3 ripe tomatoes, diced
1/4 c. low-sodium chicken or
   vegetable broth
2 T. fresh parsley, chopped
red pepper flakes to taste
Garnish: shredded Parmesan
   cheese

Cook pasta according to package directions. Drain, reserving 1/2 cup of the cooking water. Meanwhile, heat oil in a large saucepan over medium heat. Add garlic and shallots; sauté for one minute. Add zucchini and season with salt and pepper; cook for 2 minutes. Add tomatoes, broth, parsley and pepper flakes. Cook and stir for one minute; remove from heat. Add zucchini mixture to pasta and toss well, adding a little of the reserved cooking water to desired consistency. Serve with Parmesan cheese. Makes 4 servings.

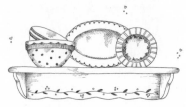

A can't-go-wrong mix of new and vintage tableware is
always a fun and different way to serve up dinner.
Go ahead and use all your favorites!

Family Dinner Favorites

Penn Dutch Corn Pie

Janice Schuler
Alburtis, PA

A Pennsylvania Dutch staple! As kids, we used to wait all summer long to eat corn on the cob. Then after two or three weeks, it seemed like we were eating it three times a day! We were never able to freeze it on the cob without it getting soggy, so this recipe was a delicious change. My favorite lunch or dinner? Corn pie, tomato sandwiches and a wedge of watermelon...I could eat that every day!

2 9-inch pie crusts, uncooked
2 to 2-1/2 c. fresh sweet corn
3/4 c. milk
1-1/4 t. salt
Optional: 3 to 4 eggs,
    hard-boiled, peeled and diced

pepper to taste
1 T. butter, diced
Optional: additional milk,
    warmed

Place one crust in a 9" pie plate. Fill crust with alternating layers of corn, milk, salt and eggs, if using. Sprinkle pepper on top; dot with butter. Cover with second pie crust and seal edges of crust together. Make several slits in top crust with a knife tip. Bake at 425 degrees for 10 minutes. Reduce heat to 325 degrees and continue to bake for 25 minutes, or until crust is golden. Serve hot, topped with additional milk, if desired. Serves 6 to 8.

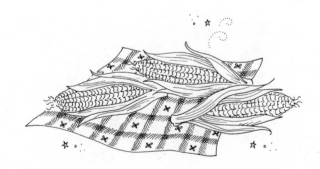

If you're substituting frozen corn for fresh kernels,
a 10-ounce package of frozen equals 1-3/4 cups fresh.

FRESH FARMHOUSE
Recipes

Garden-Stuffed Chicken Breasts

Charlene McCain
Bakersfield, CA

This is a recipe you can feel good about serving your family. It's quick to cook and clean-up is effortless, which is a big plus. A delicious dinner in under an hour is a winner in my book! Serve with seasoned rice, if you like.

3 to 4 mushrooms, sliced
1/2 c. green pepper, chopped
3/4 c. red pepper, chopped
1/2 c. onion, chopped
2 to 3 spears asparagus, chopped

2 to 3 t. olive oil
2 boneless, skinless chicken
   breasts
salt and pepper to taste

In a skillet over medium heat, toss vegetables with olive oil. Cook until onion is translucent; remove vegetables from skillet. Meanwhile, use a sharp knife to cut a slit in the side of each chicken breast, forming a pocket. Season chicken breasts with salt and pepper. Spoon cooked vegetables into pockets in chicken breasts. Add chicken breasts to hot skillet; cook for about 4 minutes per side. Arrange chicken breasts to an aluminum foil-covered 13"x9" baking pan. Bake, uncovered, at 425 degrees for about 20 minutes, until chicken juices run clear. Serves 2 to 4.

Can't get to the farmers' market early in the day? Stop by near closing time. Often, vendors will sell veggies at a discount to avoid packing the day's leftovers to take home.

Family Dinner Favorites

Roasted Tomato Spaghetti Sauce

Marlene Borges
Fresno, CA

This is a good way to use up all the extra tomatoes from the garden. Any kinds of tomatoes can be used. Serve with your favorite pasta, or spoon into plastic freezer bags to freeze and enjoy in the future.

20 tomatoes, quartered
2 onions, quartered
2 green peppers, sliced
2 to 3 cloves garlic, peeled
olive oil to taste

salt and pepper to taste
6-oz. can tomato paste
dried oregano to taste
Optional: fresh or canned sliced
   mushrooms to taste

In a large ungreased roasting pan, combine tomatoes, onions, peppers and garlic cloves. Drizzle olive oil over vegetables; season with salt and pepper. Stir gently. Bake, uncovered, at 350 degrees for one hour. Increase oven temperature to 400 degrees and bake another 20 to 30 minutes, until vegetables are darkened and soft. Transfer vegetables and juices to a stockpot; process with an immersion blender until well blended. Stir in tomato paste, oregano and mushrooms, if using; season with additional salt and pepper to taste. Bring to a boil over medium-high heat; reduce heat to medium-low. Simmer for 20 to 30 minutes, stirring occasionally. Makes 8 to 10 servings.

If you have a bumper crop of green peppers, freeze them whole... it's simple! Just wash well, slice off the tops and remove the seeds. Wrap peppers individually in aluminum foil and place in a freezer bag. Peppers can be sliced or chopped while still slightly frozen.

FRESH FARMHOUSE
Recipes

Sheet Pan Sausage, Potatoes & Brussels Sprouts

Rachel Kowasic
Valrico, FL

Growing up on a farm, we always used fresh ingredients when the season was right. This easy recipe is delicious with fresh vegetables and herbs in the mix.

16-oz. pkg. smoked pork
   sausage, sliced
5 redskin potatoes, diced
1 onion, chopped
1/2 lb. Brussels sprouts, thawed
   if frozen and halved

2 t. Dijon mustard
2 cloves garlic, minced
1/4 c. balsamic vinegar
1/4 c. olive oil
6 leaves fresh sage, chopped
salt and pepper to taste

In a large bowl, combine sausage, potatoes, onion and Brussels sprouts; set aside. Whisk together remaining ingredients in another bowl; pour over sausage mixture and toss to mix well. Spread mixture evenly on an aluminum foil-covered baking sheet. Bake at 400 degrees for about 25 to 30 minutes, until sausage is browned and potatoes are soft and starting to brown. Stir; broil for about 5 minutes, to crisp up a bit more. Makes 4 to 6 servings.

It's easy to dry fresh herbs…just bunch them together with kitchen twine and hang upside-down. Once they're dry, you can enjoy the flavor of garden-fresh herbs no matter what the season.

Family Dinner Favorites

Layered Meatloaf

Diana Krol
Hutchinson, KS

This cheese-topped meatloaf is delicious! I like to serve it with baked potatoes, green beans and an apple crisp. Everything can be baked together in the oven at the same time.

1 lb. ground beef
1 egg, beaten
1/2 onion, chopped
2/3 c. rolled oats, uncooked
1/2 c. chicken broth
1/4 c. grated Parmesan cheese
1/4 c. catsup

1 t. Worcestershire sauce
poultry seasoning, salt and
  pepper to taste
1 c. shredded sharp Cheddar
  cheese
1/2 c. barbecue sauce

In a large bowl, mix together all ingredients except shredded cheese and barbecue sauce. Gently pat half of beef mixture into a greased 9"x5" loaf pan. Layer with cheese and remaining beef mixture; brush barbecue sauce on top. Bake, uncovered, at 350 degrees for one hour. Slice to serve. Serves 4 to 6.

Mashed potatoes are the perfect partner for meatloaf. Peel potatoes, cut into chunks and cook in boiling water until fork-tender, 10 to 20 minutes. Drain, mash right in the pot and stir in butter, salt and a little milk to desired consistency. Yummy!

121

FRESH FARMHOUSE
Recipes

Rigatoni with Green Tomatoes
Eleanor Dionne
Beverly, MA

We make this dish whenever we have an overabundance of tomatoes. It's delicious and a little different! Fresh herbs make it special.

1 T. canola oil
3/4 c. onion, finely chopped
1 t. garlic, finely chopped
4 c. green tomatoes, thinly sliced
1/4 to 1/2 c. chicken broth
1-1/2 T. fresh basil, coarsely chopped

1 T. fresh parsley, finely chopped
salt and pepper to taste
8-oz. pkg. rigatoni pasta, uncooked
3 T. grated Parmesan cheese
Garnish: additional chopped fresh parsley

Heat oil in a large skillet over medium heat; add onion and sauté until golden. Add garlic and cook for one minute. Add tomatoes and simmer for 5 minutes, stirring occasionally. Add 1/4 cup chicken broth, fresh herbs, salt and pepper. Cover and simmer for 20 minutes, adding more broth if needed. Meanwhile, cook pasta according to package directions; drain well. Add pasta to sauce; toss to coat well. Add cheese; mix well and and serve. Garnish with additional parsley. Makes 4 servings.

Drive into the country and go stargazing! The best times to watch for shooting stars occur in April, August, October and November, but any clear night will provide a world of wonder overhead...you might even spot the Milky Way!

Family Dinner Favorites

Chicken & Broccoli Vermicelli

Amy Thomason Hunt
Traphill, NC

I first tried this dish at a friend's house while my husband was stationed at Camp LeJeune in the U.S. Marine Corps. Needless to say, I had to have the recipe! It's simple comfort food.

4 boneless, skinless chicken
  breasts
14-oz. can chicken broth
8-oz. pkg. vermicelli pasta,
  uncooked
10-oz. pkg. frozen chopped
  broccoli, cooked

10-3/4 oz. can cream of chicken
  soup
5/8 c. milk
12-oz. pkg. pasteurized process
  cheese, cubed and melted

Cover chicken with water in a stockpot. Bring to a boil over high heat; reduce to medium-low. Simmer until chicken is tender and juices run clear. Remove chicken to a platter; reserve cooking liquid in stockpot. Cut chicken into bite-size chunks; set aside. Add canned chicken broth to reserved cooking liquid and bring to a boil. Add pasta and cook according to package directions. Drain, reserving 1-1/4 cups broth mixture. In a lightly greased 13"x9" baking pan, combine chicken, cooked vermicelli, broccoli, soup, reserved broth, milk and cheese. Mix gently. Bake, uncovered, at 350 degrees for 30 minutes, or until bubbly and golden. Serves 8 to 10.

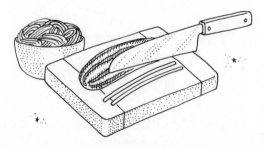

For a delicious, healthy change from regular pasta, make "zoodles." Cut zucchini into long, thin strips, steam lightly or sauté in a little olive oil and toss with your favorite pasta sauce. Works with yellow squash too!

FRESH FARMHOUSE
Recipes

Easy Roast Chicken

Aqsa Masood
Ontario, Canada

I came up with this simple recipe for my family because they just love roast chicken. It is so easy, anyone can cook it! With just a few simple pantry ingredients, you can enjoy a really simple but flavorful meal with your loved ones. My children love it with mint chutney, French fries and pita bread. Or serve with roasted veggies and garlic bread.

3 to 3-1/2 lb. whole chicken
6 T. butter, melted
2 T. canola oil
1/2 t. meat tenderizer powder

1/2 t. garlic powder
1/2 t. onion powder
1/2 t. dry mustard
1/2 t. pepper

Place chicken in a roasting pan; set aside. Combine remaining ingredients in a bowl; gently brush or rub on and under the chicken skin. If desired, refrigerate for one hour before baking. Bake, uncovered, at 400 degrees for 30 minutes. Reduce oven temperature to 375 degrees; bake for one hour, or until chicken juices run clear. For a softer skin, baste chicken with pan drippings while baking; omit if a crispy skin is preferred. Let stand at room temperature for several minutes; slice and serve. Serves 5 to 6.

Make your own flavorful chicken broth. Freeze roast chicken bones and when you have the bones from 2 to 3 chickens saved, place them in a large slow cooker. Add some chopped carrots, celery and onion; cover with water. Cover and cook on low setting for 8 to 10 hours. Strain broth and pour into recipe-size containers; refrigerate or freeze.

Family Dinner Favorites

Eggplant Deluxe

Michele Feis
West Islip, NY

One day, time was short and I had some eggplant cutlets already breaded and fried, so I layered my extra ingredients and baked. Everyone loved it!

2 Italian eggplants, peeled
   and sliced 1/4-inch thick
2 eggs, beaten
2 c. dry bread crumbs
oil for frying
28-oz. can crushed tomatoes,
   drained

15-oz. can tomato sauce
15-oz. container ricotta cheese
8-oz. pkg. shredded mozzarella
   cheese

Dip eggplant slices into egg, then into crumbs. Heat 1/4-inch oil in a skillet over medium-high heat. Cook eggplant slices until golden on both sides. Meanwhile, simmer tomatoes and tomato sauce in a saucepan over medium heat until slightly thickened. Making one or 2 layers, arrange slices in a greased 13"x9" baking pan. Add a dollop of ricotta cheese to each slice; top with mozzarella cheese. Spoon tomato mixture over top. Bake, uncovered, at 350 degrees for 30 minutes, or until bubbly and eggplant is tender. Serves 6.

Unstuffed Cabbage

Cheryie Wilson
Port Richey, FL

This recipe is so much easier than stuffed cabbage, with the same great taste. Serve with some hot crusty bread to sop up the juices...yum!

1 lb. ground beef
10-3/4 oz. can tomato soup
1 c. water
1 c. instant rice, uncooked

16-oz. pkg. shredded cabbage
2 T. dried, minced onions
salt and pepper to taste

Brown beef in a large skillet over medium heat; drain. Whisk in soup and water until blended; stir in remaining ingredients. Reduce heat to medium-low. Simmer for about 20 minutes, stirring occasionally, until cabbage is tender. Serves 4.

FRESH FARMHOUSE
Recipes

Grandma's Luncheon Dish
Marla Kinnersley
Surprise, AZ

Grandma made this recipe often for her family. I'm not sure where she got it, but it's been in our family for years. It was a family favorite through the generations and we all continue to make it for our families today. True comfort food at its finest!

16-oz. pkg. elbow macaroni, uncooked	2 10-3/4 oz. cans tomato soup
1 lb. ground beef	15-oz. can corn, drained
1 yellow onion, chopped	4 slices American cheese, cut up
1 green pepper, chopped	1 t. salt
	1/2 t. pepper

Cook macaroni according to package directions; drain. Meanwhile, brown beef with onion and green pepper in a large skillet over medium heat; drain. Add soup, corn, cheese, salt and pepper; heat through. Add cooked macaroni; stir until well combined. Serves 8.

Summer Stew
Michelle Powell
Valley, AL

In summer, I like to make this fresh-tasting stew with the summer garden's bounty. In the winter, I use canned tomatoes and frozen veggies for a hearty supper with cornbread.

4 slices bacon	1/2 c. chicken broth
2 onions, thinly sliced	2 T. sugar
2 lbs. fresh okra, sliced	2 t. catsup
1 lb. fresh sweet corn	1 t. lemon pepper seasoning
2 lbs. ripe tomatoes, quartered	

Cook bacon in a large skillet over medium heat. Drain bacon on paper towels, reserving drippings. Sauté onions in reserved drippings. Add okra and corn; sauté about 5 minutes. Add tomatoes, crumbled bacon and remaining ingredients. Cover and simmer over medium-low heat for one hour, stirring occasionally. Makes 6 servings.

Family Dinner Favorites

Chicken & Vegetable Skillet

Cindy Neel
Gooseberry Patch

We love this hearty dish! It's really simple to put together...ready to serve in no time. Feel free to mix & match your favorite veggies.

2 T. olive oil
1-1/4 lbs. boneless, skinless
   chicken breasts, cut into
   strips
1 c. green beans or asparagus,
   cut into 2-inch pieces
1 c. zucchini or yellow squash,
   thinly sliced

1/2 c. green pepper, sliced
1/2 c. onion, sliced
2 t. Italian seasoning
2 t. seasoned salt
1 c. red or yellow cherry
   tomatoes
Optional: shredded Parmesan
   cheese

Heat oil in a large skillet over medium-high heat; add chicken strips. Cook and stir for 5 to 6 minutes, until golden. Add vegetables except tomatoes and seasonings. Cook and stir for 5 minutes, until vegetables are tender-crisp. Add tomatoes; cook and stir for one to 2 minutes, until tomatoes are slightly softened and chicken is cooked through. Serve topped with cheese, if desired. Makes 6 servings.

Invite friends to join you for a favorite skillet or casserole supper...a meal shared with friends doesn't need to be fancy. After all, it's friendship that makes it special!

FRESH FARMHOUSE
Recipes

Halibut with Tomatoes & Zucchini in Foil

Vickie
Gooseberry Patch

We love to cook on the grill in the summertime! This recipe makes a delicious lighter meal that we enjoy. Serve with a tossed salad and warm buttered rolls.

2 to 3 zucchini, quartered and
   cut into 1-inch pieces
2 c. cherry tomatoes
1/4 c. pitted Kalamata olives,
   halved
4 6-oz. skinless halibut fillets,
   thawed if frozen

salt and pepper to taste
2 cloves garlic, thinly sliced
4 sprigs fresh rosemary
2 T. olive oil
Garnish: lemon wedges

Lay out 4 pieces heavy-duty aluminum foil, each 12 inches long. Divide zucchini, tomatoes and olives evenly among foil pieces; top with halibut fillets. Season fish with salt and pepper. Top fish evenly with garlic and a rosemary sprig; drizzle with oil. Fold sides of foil over fish and vegetables to cover completely; crimp edges to seal packets. Preheat a grill over medium-high heat; arrange packets on grill. Cook, turning packets once, for 10 to 12 minutes, until vegetables are sizzling inside packets and fish flakes easily. Open packets carefully; serve with lemon wedges. Serves 4.

For mild, fresh-tasting fish, place frozen fillets in a shallow dish, cover with milk and let thaw overnight in the fridge.

Family Dinner Favorites

Baked Tuna Cakes

Jill Ball
Highland, UT

Whenever I have forgotten to thaw something and need dinner quick, this is one of my go-to recipes. It's yummy, fast and healthier than regular fried tuna cakes.

1 sleeve saltine crackers, crushed
2 6-1/2 oz. cans tuna in water
2 egg whites
1 T. soy sauce
1/4 t. garlic powder
6 T. red, yellow and/or green peppers, finely diced

Place crushed crackers in a bowl. Add undrained tuna, egg whites, soy sauce and garlic powder; mix until well blended. Add peppers and stir until well mixed. Form evenly into 8 flattened patties; arrange on a lightly greased baking sheet. Bake at 350 degrees for 8 minutes and turn over. Bake for another 8 minutes. Serves 4.

Lemon-Dill Salmon

Carolyn Gochenaur
Howe, IN

Whenever I go up to my sister Debbie's home in Minnesota, I ask her to make this for me. It's quick, easy, and good! If there's any left over, she likes to add a little chopped onion, mayonnaise, sugar, salt and pepper to make a tasty spread for crackers or party bread.

3-1/2 to 4-lb. salmon fillet
1/4 c. butter, softened
1/4 c. lemon juice
2 t. dill weed
1 t. lemon pepper seasoning
Garnish: lemon wedges

Place salmon in a buttered 13"x9" baking pan; set aside. Combine remaining ingredients in a small bowl; spread over salmon. Cover loosely with aluminum foil. Bake at 450 degrees for 17 to 20 minutes; do not overbake. Serve with lemon wedges. Serves 8 to 10.

Start family meals with a gratitude circle...each person takes a moment to share something that he or she is thankful for that day. It's a sure way to put everyone in a cheerful mood!

FRESH FARMHOUSE
Recipes

Turkey Zucchini Boats

Maria Kuhns
Crofton, MD

I love to experiment with recipes, and this healthy sheet-pan version gives you all the best of Italian flavors with none of the guilt. Serve with fresh fruit for a wonderful meal.

2 T. olive oil, divided
1 lb. ground turkey
3/4 c. onion, finely diced
1 red pepper, finely diced
1 green pepper, finely diced
1/2 t. dried basil
1/2 t. dried oregano
1/2 t. dried parsley
1/2 t. dried thyme

1/2 t. garlic powder
1/2 t. onion powder
1/2 to 1 t. red pepper flakes
salt and pepper to taste
14-oz. jar marinara sauce
6 zucchini, halved lengthwise
1 c. shredded low-fat mozzarella
cheese

Heat one tablespoon olive oil in a medium skillet. Add turkey and cook until no longer pink; drain and set aside. To another skillet, add remaining olive oil, onion, peppers and seasonings. Sauté until onion is transparent and peppers are soft, about 5 minutes. Stir in turkey and marinara sauce; simmer over low heat until heated through. Scoop pulp out of zucchini halves, leaving a hollow shell. Mound turkey in shells; top with cheese and arrange on an aluminum foil-lined rimmed baking sheet. Bake at 350 degrees for 30 minutes, until bubbly and zucchini shells are fork-tender. Makes 6 servings.

Tuck fresh blossoms into vintage glass soda bottles
to line up on a windowsill.

Family Dinner Favorites

Easy Pasta & Broccoli Alfredo

Cinde Shields
Issaquah, WA

This is an easy weeknight meal that my whole family can agree on!
It couldn't be simpler to prepare this rich and creamy pasta dish.
Cooking the broccoli in the same pot as the pasta means one less
pan to wash.

16-oz. pkg. medium pasta shells, uncooked
4 c. broccoli flowerets
8-oz. pkg. cream cheese, cubed
2 c. milk
1/2 c. butter
1/2 t. pepper
8-oz. pkg. shredded Parmesan cheese, divided
Optional: nutmeg to taste

Cook pasta according to package directions; add broccoli to pasta pot during last 5 minutes of cooktime (for tender broccoli) or 3 minutes (for crisp-tender broccoli). Drain; place in a large serving bowl. Meanwhile, in a saucepan, combine cream cheese, milk and butter. Cook and stir over low heat until well blended and cream cheese is completely melted. Stir in pepper and one cup Parmesan cheese. Add cream cheese mixture to pasta mixture; mix lightly. Sprinkle with remaining Parmesan cheese. Sprinkle lightly with nutmeg, if desired. Serves 4 to 6.

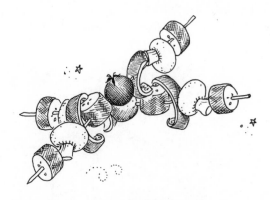

Grill some tasty veggie kabobs. Toss sliced peppers, mushrooms, zucchini, sweet onion and cherry tomatoes with a drizzle of olive oil. Thread onto skewers and season with salt & pepper. Grill over medium heat, turning after about 5 minutes, until tender.

FRESH FARMHOUSE
Recipes

Macaroni-Stuffed Green Peppers

Thomas Hiegel
Union City, OH

I don't care for rice, so I use macaroni. Try this recipe and I think you'll enjoy it.

4 green peppers, tops removed
1 lb. ground beef
1/4 c. sweet onion, chopped
1/4 c. celery, chopped
1 c. cooked elbow macaroni
1/2 t. salt
1/8 t. white pepper

2 8-oz. cans tomato sauce, divided
1 t. sugar
1/4 t. dried basil
1/2 c. shredded mozzarella cheese

Cut peppers in half lengthwise; add to a large saucepan of boiling water. Cook for 5 minutes. Drain; set aside. Meanwhile, in a large skillet over medium heat, brown beef with onion and celery; drain. Add cooked macaroni, salt, pepper and one can tomato sauce to beef mixture; mix well. Spoon mixture into pepper halves; arrange peppers in a shallow baking pan and set aside. In a bowl, combine remaining can of tomato sauce, sugar and basil; mix well. Spoon half of sauce mixture over peppers. Bake, uncovered, at 350 degrees for 30 to 40 minutes, until peppers are fork-tender. Spoon remaining sauce over peppers; sprinkle with cheese. Bake another 5 minutes, or until cheese is melted. Makes 4 servings.

Tie ruffled vintage aprons onto the backs of kitchen chairs for a sweet welcome to a country-style supper.

Family Dinner Favorites

Cheesy Brats One-Pot Meal

Samantha Starks
Madison, WI

My hubby really enjoys this one-dish recipe! Just add a basket of hot rolls for a great meal.

6 bratwursts or Polish sausages, sliced 1/2-inch thick
4 potatoes, peeled, cubed and cooked
1 lb. fresh green beans, trimmed and steamed
10-3/4 oz. can cream of mushroom soup
1 c. shredded Cheddar cheese
1/3 c. onion, chopped
garlic powder, salt and pepper to taste
Optional: additional Cheddar cheese

Combine all ingredients in a lightly greased 3-quart casserole dish. Stir gently. Cover and bake at 350 degrees for about 45 minutes, until hot and bubbly. If desired, top with more cheese; let stand until melted. Serves 6 to 8.

Prefer to shred cheese yourself? Shred it in a jiffy.
Freeze wrapped cheese for 10 to 20 minutes...it will
just glide across the grater!

FRESH FARMHOUSE
Recipes

Zucchini Veggie Beef Ragout
Nancy Swecker
Elizabethton, TN

Curry powder and lemon pepper seasoning give this low-carb dish some zing, and with plenty of veggies, it's extra satisfying.

1 lb. ground beef	3 c. eggplant, diced
1 c. onion, chopped	1 c. sliced mushrooms
1 t. garlic, minced	Optional: 1/4 c. beef broth
1 t. salt	or water
1/4 t. pepper	1 t. lemon pepper seasoning
3 c. zucchini, diced	3/8 t. curry powder

In a large skillet over medium heat, cook beef with onion, garlic, salt and pepper until beef is no longer pink. Drain. Add zucchini, eggplant and mushrooms; stir-fry until vegetables are tender. Add broth or water if mixture starts to stick to the pan. Stir in seasonings and serve. Makes 4 to 6 servings.

Small-town festivals are full of old-fashioned fun...where else could you eat a pumpkin burger or cheer on an antique tractor pull? Check with your state's tourism office for a list of seasonal festivals and fairs in your area, then pick one and go!

Family Dinner Favorites

Fettuccine with Mushrooms & Peas

Wendy Perry
Midland, VA

My husband loves fettuccine and does not miss the calories in this creamy delight!

12-oz. pkg. whole-wheat
   fettuccine, uncooked
1 T. olive oil
3 to 4 c. cremini or baby
   portabella mushrooms, sliced
3 c. frozen peas, thawed
Optional: 1 shallot, minced
1 T. garlic, minced

1/2 c. dry sherry or water
2 T. all-purpose flour
2 c. 2% milk
1/2 t. salt
1/2 t. pepper
1 c. shredded Asiago or
   Parmesan cheese

Cook pasta according to package directions; drain and transfer to a serving dish. Meanwhile, heat oil in a large skillet over medium heat. Add mushrooms, peas and shallot, if using; cook for 10 minutes. Add garlic; cook and stir for one minute. Add sherry or water and bring to a boil; scraping up any browned bits in bottom of pan. In a bowl, mix together flour, milk, salt and pepper and add to skillet. Cook and stir until thickened, about 2 minutes. To serve, spoon sauce over pasta and top with cheese. Serves 6.

The secret to perfectly cooked pasta is to use plenty of cooking water…about a gallon per pound of pasta, in a very large pot.

FRESH FARMHOUSE
Recipes

Nancy's Meatball Stew

Nancy Kaiser
York, SC

This stew is great on a cold day, served with homemade bread or rolls and butter. It warms the belly and the soul.

1 lb. lean ground beef
1/2 c. onion, finely chopped
2 eggs, beaten
1 t. dried parsley
1 t. lemon juice
1/2 t. mustard
1/2 t. salt
4 c. boiling water

4 cubes beef bouillon
2 T. molasses
4 t. soy sauce
3 to 4 potatoes, peeled and cubed
2 to 3 carrots, peeled and sliced
1/2 c. onion, coarsely chopped
1 c. cold water
1/2 c. all-purpose flour

In a large bowl, combine beef, finely chopped onion, eggs, parsley, lemon juice, mustard and salt. Mix well; shape into 1-1/2 inch balls and brown in a large skillet over medium heat. Meanwhile, in a saucepan, combine boiling water and bouillon cubes; let stand until dissolved. Stir in molasses and soy sauce; pour broth mixture over meatballs. Add potatoes, carrots and coarsely chopped onion. Cover and simmer over medium heat until vegetables are tender. Whisk together cold water and flour; add to meatball mixture. Cook and stir until thickened. Serves 4 to 6.

When browning meatballs, you'll get the best results if the pan isn't overcrowded. Use an extra-large skillet, or cook in 2 batches.

Family Dinner Favorites

Chicken & Mushrooms

Leona Krivda
Belle Vernon, PA

When I made this recipe for the first time, my hubby loved it! He asked me to please make this again, soon. I had to laugh because it's so easy!

3 T. butter, divided
2 boneless, skinless chicken
    breasts
salt and pepper to taste
1/2 lb. sliced mushrooms
1/4 c. water

1/4 c. whipping cream
1 t. lemon juice
3 c. fresh baby spinach, stems
    removed
garlic powder and/or turmeric
    to taste

Melt one tablespoon butter in a skillet over medium heat. Add chicken; cook until golden on both sides and cooked through. Remove chicken to a plate; season with salt and pepper on both sides. Melt remaining butter in same skillet; add mushrooms and cook until tender. Stir in water, cream and lemon juice; simmer over low heat until sauce thickens. Stir in spinach and desired seasonings. Place chicken pieces on top; spoon some sauce over chicken. Serve chicken with sauce mixture. Serves 2.

Take it easy on alternate Friday nights...arrange for a neighborly dinner swap! One week, you make a double batch of a favorite casserole and deliver one to a friend. Next week, she returns the favor. You're sure to discover some great new recipes while gaining a little free time too.

FRESH FARMHOUSE
Recipes

Mom's Chicken Pot Pies

Hollie Moots
Marysville, OH

Pure comfort food! This is one of my family's most-requested dinners. I've even been known to double the recipe to make enough for my grown kids to put in their freezers. Then they can have a little taste of home anytime! If you have a vegetarian in the family, make the base with vegetable broth and set aside a bowlfull before adding the chicken.

2 c. potatoes, peeled and diced	1-3/4 c. milk
1-1/2 c. carrots, peeled and diced	1 c. frozen peas
1 c. butter	1 c. frozen corn
1 c. onions, chopped	4 c. chicken, cooked and cubed
1 c. all-purpose flour	14.1-oz. pkg. refrigerated pie
1 t. dried thyme	crusts, unbaked
2 t. salt	1 egg, beaten
1 t. pepper	1 to 2 t. water
3 c. chicken or vegetable broth	

Add potatoes and carrots to a saucepan; cover with water. Bring to a boil over high heat. Boil for 10 minutes, or just until vegetables are tender; drain and set aside. In a separate large saucepan, melt butter over medium-high heat. Add onions and sauté until tender, about 5 minutes. Sprinkle with flour and seasonings; cook and stir for 2 minutes, or until thick and bubbly. Reduce heat to medium. Gradually stir in broth and milk. Stir in potato mixture, peas, corn and chicken. Ladle filling into 6 oven-safe soup bowls. Roll out pie crusts; cut into 6 circles the size of the bowl openings. Top each bowl with a circle of crust. Mix beaten egg and water; brush over crust. Cut several slashes into each crust with a knife tip. Bake at 400 degrees for 30 to 45 minutes, until bubbly and crust is golden. Serves 6.

Quick & easy farmhouse napkin rings! Glue a charm or button to a little grapevine ring and tuck in a cloth napkin.

Family Dinner Favorites

Vegetable Risotto

Mary Bettuchy
Saint Robert, MO

A delicious meatless dish you're sure to love! Be sure to keep the broth hot while this is cooking, so that it doesn't cool down the rice each time it is added to the pot. Sometimes I vary it according to the season and what I have available in my garden. In late summer, I may toss in some cherry tomatoes and green beans. For a little different flavor, I'll add lime juice and zest instead of lemon.

6 c. chicken or vegetable broth
2 T. olive oil
1/2 c. onion, diced
1 clove garlic, minced
3 c. arborio rice, uncooked
1 c. white wine or chicken or
    vegetable broth

2 c. asparagus tips
1 c. snow peas
2 c. yellow squash, sliced
5 to 6 radishes, thinly sliced
3/4 c. grated Parmesan cheese
zest and juice of one lemon
salt and pepper to taste

In a large saucepan, heat broth over medium-high heat to nearly boiling; reduce heat to a simmer. Meanwhile, in a Dutch oven over medium heat, heat olive oil until shimmering. Add onion to oil and sauté for about 5 minutes, until translucent and softened. Add garlic and sauté for one minute more. Add rice and sauté for about 2 minutes. Add wine or broth and cook about 30 seconds, stirring constantly. Add 2 cups of hot broth; reduce heat to medium-low. Cook, uncovered, stirring occasionally, until most of the liquid has been absorbed. Add asparagus tips, snow peas, squash and 2 more cups hot broth; simmer until most of the liquid has been absorbed. Add remaining hot broth and radishes; simmer until all liquid has been absorbed. Remove from heat. Stir in cheese, lemon zest and juice; season with salt and pepper. Serves 4 to 6.

Try serving a meatless main once a week...it's economical and healthy too. There are lots of tasty rice and vegetable-based dishes to choose from.

FRESH FARMHOUSE
Recipes

Beer-Battered Fried Fish

Robin Scott
Grayson, KY

This is our favorite fried fish recipe. We think it tastes just as good as any commercial seafood restaurant's fried fish, only better! Tilapia is a good fish choice, but any mild white fish will work.

1 lb. tilapia or other fish fillets
2 c. all-purpose flour, divided
1 t. baking powder
1/2 t. salt
1 egg, lightly beaten

12-oz. bottle regular or
   non-alcoholic beer
1/4 c. oil
oil for deep frying

In a shallow dish, coat fish fillets with one cup flour; shake off excess flour and set aside. In a large bowl, combine remaining flour, baking powder, salt, egg, beer and 1/4 cup oil; beat until smooth. Dip fish into batter, allowing excess batter to drip into bowl. Attach a deep-frying thermometer to the side of a heavy 3-quart saucepan. Add 2 inches oil to pan; heat to about 375 degrees over high heat. Add fish, several pieces at a time, and cook until golden, about 4 to 5 minutes per side. Drain on paper towels. Serves 4.

Mix up a bowl of pineapple coleslaw in a jiffy...delicious with fried chicken or fish! Combine a package of shredded coleslaw mix and your favorite coleslaw dressing, adding dressing to taste. Stir in some drained pineapple tidbits for a sweet twist.

Family Dinner Favorites

Crispy Fried Chicken

Wendy Jo Minotte
Duluth, MN

This recipe tastes great hot or cold! I love to serve it with homemade fries in red plastic baskets lined with red-checked paper napkins. Makes a home-cooked meal look fancy and everyone loves it!

4 lbs. chicken drumsticks
    or tenders
1/2 t. salt
1/2 t. pepper
1 egg, lightly beaten

1/4 c. milk
3/4 c. all-purpose flour
1 t. cayenne pepper
canola oil for frying

Season chicken with salt and pepper; set aside. Whisk together egg and milk in a shallow dish; combine flour and cayenne pepper in another shallow dish. Dip chicken into egg mixture and dredge in flour mixture, coating well. Pour oil to a depth of one inch in a heavy cast-iron skillet; heat oil to 350 degrees. Working in batches, cook chicken in hot oil over medium-high heat for 15 to 20 minutes, until golden and chicken juices run clear, turning every 5 minutes. Drain on paper towels. Serves 6.

Seasoned Baked Pork Chops

Kristin Pittis
Dennison, OH

The spicy-sweet dry rub makes these pork chops delicious! They are quick-cooking and perfect for a 30-minute weeknight meal.

2 T. brown sugar, packed
1 t. salt
1 t. chili powder
1/2 t. garlic powder

1/2 t. onion powder
1/2 t. paprika
4 boneless pork chops
2 T. butter, sliced

Combine brown sugar and seasonings in a shallow dish. Press pork chops into seasoning mixture on both sides, shaking off excess. Place pork chops on a parchment paper or aluminum foil-lined baking sheet. Top each pork chop with a pat of butter. Bake, uncovered, at 425 degrees for 20 to 25 minutes. Makes 4 servings.

FRESH FARMHOUSE
Recipes

Baked Pasta Primavera & Sausage

Mia Rossi
Charlotte, NC

My family enjoys my Pasta Primavera that's chock-full of garden vegetables, but they want a little more for dinner, so I added some sausage. Feel free to use your favorite flavor of sausage and mix & match the veggies!

1/2 lb. mushrooms, quartered
2 c. cherry tomatoes, halved
3/4 c. onion, chopped
1 zucchini, sliced
1 red or yellow pepper, chopped
1/4 c. olive oil
1/4 t. salt
1/8 t. pepper
12-oz. pkg. smoked pork or
    chicken sausage link, sliced
12-oz. pkg. penne pasta,
    uncooked
Garnish: shredded Parmesan
    cheese

In a large bowl, combine vegetables, oil, salt and pepper. Toss to coat; spread evenly on a shallow greased 13"x9" baking pan. Bake, uncovered, at 400 degrees for 30 minutes, stirring occasionally, or until vegetables are tender and lightly golden. Arrange sausage slices over vegetables. Return to oven for 5 minutes, or until sausage is heated through. Meanwhile, cook pasta according to package directions; drain and place in a large bowl. Add sausage mixture; toss. Sprinkle with cheese and serve. Serves 4 to 6.

Invite friends and neighbors to a good old-fashioned block party. Set up picnic tables, arrange lots of chairs in the shade and invite everyone to bring a favorite dish. Whether it's a summer cookout or a fall harvest party, you'll make some wonderful memories together!

Family Dinner Favorites

Spinach & Artichoke Stuffed Shells

Shirley Howie
Foxboro, MA

If you like spinach & artichoke dip, you will love these stuffed shells! They're really good...a great vegetarian alternative to traditional meat-stuffed shells. They are always a hit at potluck dinners and can be made ahead and reheated.

18 jumbo pasta shells, uncooked
15-oz. container ricotta cheese
1 c. shredded Swiss cheese
10-oz. pkg. frozen chopped
    spinach, thawed and drained

6-oz. jar marinated artichoke
    hearts, drained
1/4 t. nutmeg
2 c. marinara pasta sauce
1 c. grated Parmesan cheese

Cook pasta shells according to package directions, just until tender; drain. Meanwhile, in a large bowl, combine ricotta cheese, Swiss cheese, spinach, artichokes and nutmeg; mix well. Spoon mixture into cooked pasta shells; arrange in a 13"x9" baking pan coated with non-stick vegetable spray. Spoon marinara sauce over stuffed shells; sprinkle with Parmesan cheese. Cover pan tightly with aluminum foil. Bake for 40 minutes at 375 degrees. Uncover pan and bake 10 minutes longer, or until bubbly and cheese is golden. Makes 6 to 9 servings, 2 to 3 shells each.

What if the recipe is farmhouse-size and your family is small? Simple...just divide the casserole ingredients into 2 small dishes and freeze one for later!

FRESH FARMHOUSE
Recipes

Beefy Mushroom Mac

Jodi Spires
Centerville, OH

*Great comfort food! Fast and easy to prepare with
ingredients you probably already have on hand.*

8-oz. pkg. elbow macaroni,
  uncooked
1 lb. ground beef chuck
1/2 c. onion, diced
2 10-3/4 oz. cans cream of
  mushroom soup

1 c. milk
1/2 c. sour cream
salt and pepper to taste
8-oz. pkg. shredded Cheddar
  cheese

Cook macaroni according to package directions, just until tender; drain.
Meanwhile, brown beef with onion in a skillet over medium heat;
drain. In a large bowl, whisk soup with milk; add sour cream and stir to
combine. Add cooked macaroni and beef mixture to bowl. Season with
salt and pepper; stir well to combine. Transfer mixture to a 3-quart
casserole dish coated with non-stick vegetable spray. Top with cheese.
Bake, uncovered, at 350 degrees for 30 minutes, or until bubbly and
cheese is melted. Let stand 5 minutes before serving. Serves 6 to 8.

For baked casseroles, cook pasta or macaroni for the shortest
cooking time recommended on the package. It's not necessary
to rinse the cooked pasta, just drain well.

Family Dinner Favorites

Barbecue Country-Style Ribs
Ann Davis
Brookville, IN

Slow cooking makes these ribs delicious and fall-apart tender!

2 c. apple juice
1/4 c. brown sugar, packed
1-1/2 t. dried, minced garlic
1 t. dried, minced onions
1/4 t. salt

1/2 t. pepper
2-1/2 lbs. country-style boneless
  pork ribs, cut into serving-
  size portions
1-1/2 c. favorite barbecue sauce

In a 5-quart slow cooker, combine all ingredients except ribs and barbecue sauce; mix well. Add ribs; stir to coat. Cover and cook on low setting for 7 to 8 hours. Remove ribs to a platter; discard liquid in slow cooker. Return ribs to slow cooker; top with barbecue sauce. Cover and cook an additional 30 minutes. Serves 5.

Fresh Tomato & Steak Dinner
Marilyn Moseley
Oldtown, ID

When I tweaked this recipe for Swiss Steak, my family loved the new twist even better than the original recipe! The twist is so simple. Adding fresh homegrown tomatoes instead of cooked ones takes this dish to happy tummy-land. Serve with hot crusty French bread and a green salad for a wonderful meal.

8 Yukon Gold potatoes, diced
3 carrots, peeled and diced
1 stalk celery, diced
3 ripe tomatoes, quartered
1 lb. beef round steak, cubed
1 t. dried basil

1 t. dried oregano
1 t. dried thyme
salt and pepper to taste
10-3/4 oz. can cream of
  mushroom soup

In a 5-quart slow cooker, layer vegetables as listed; top with steak. Sprinkle with seasonings; spoon soup over all and stir to mix. Cover and cook on low setting for 8 hours, or on high setting for 3 to 4 hours. Stir just before serving; season with additional salt and pepper, if desired. Serves 6.

FRESH FARMHOUSE
Recipes

Eggplant Lasagna

Cheryl Culver
Coyle, OK

If you love Italian food like I do, then you know this is comfort food. This is my vegetarian version of my lasagna...try and see if you agree it's a favorite too! You can add zucchini or yellow squash cut into thin strips, finely chopped broccoli or cauliflower and sweet peppers, too.

9 lasagna noodles, uncooked
1 T. olive oil
1-1/2 lbs. eggplant, thinly sliced
1/2 c. onion, chopped
3 to 4 cloves garlic, minced
1 lb. sliced mushrooms
15-1/2 oz. jar spaghetti sauce, divided

8-oz. container ricotta cheese, divided
1 c. shredded mozzarella cheese, divided
1 T. grated Parmesan cheese, divided

Cook lasagna noodles according to package directions, just until tender; drain. Meanwhile, drizzle olive oil into a large non-stick skillet over medium heat. Add eggplant slices and cook until golden on both sides; set aside eggplant. Add onion and garlic to skillet and cook for about 3 minutes, stirring occasionally. Add mushrooms; cook about 5 to 7 minutes, until tender, stirring often. Spread 1/4 of spaghetti sauce in the bottom of a greased 11"x7" baking pan. Layer 1/3 each of cooked noodles, ricotta cheese, mushroom mixture, mozzarella cheese, eggplant slices, sauce and Parmesan cheese. Repeat layers twice. Bake, uncovered, at 350 degrees for 30 to 40 minutes, until bubbly and cheese is melted. Let stand several minutes before slicing. Serves 8.

For a bountiful country-style centerpiece, heap seasonal produce in a wooden bowl...shiny sweet peppers, eggplant and zucchini in summer, acorn squash and gourds in autumn.

Family Dinner Favorites

Chicken, Squash & Dumpling Bake

Pamela Jones-Thompson
Fredericksburg, VA

My husband plants a garden every summer and we have an abundance of squash. He does all the picking and I don't mind the cooking. I hand off squash to everyone and we still have plenty left over. By trial & error I make up my own squash recipes that I think children and adults would like. This casserole is a cross between mac & cheese and chicken & dumplings, with an added wholesome bonus...squash!

8-oz. pkg. dumpling egg noodles, uncooked
2 chicken breasts, cooked and chopped or shredded
3 yellow squash, sliced
1/4 c. grated Parmesan cheese
2 10-3/4 oz. cans cream of chicken soup
1 c. water
8-oz. pkg. shredded mild or sharp Cheddar cheese

In a large bowl, combine uncooked dumplings and remaining ingredients except Cheddar cheese; mix well. Transfer to a lightly greased 12"x8" baking pan; cover with aluminum foil. Bake at 350 degrees for 30 minutes. Remove from oven; top with Cheddar cheese. Bake for 5 more minutes, or until cheese is melted. Let stand 10 to 15 minutes before serving. Serves 6 to 8.

You know, farming looks mighty easy when your plow is a pencil and you're a thousand miles from the cornfield.
—Dwight D. Eisenhower

FRESH FARMHOUSE
Recipes

Salad in a Sandwich

Lawrie Currin
Dillon, SC

This is good for an on-the-go meal...no utensils are needed!
You may substitute the bread and salad dressing as desired.

4 slices whole-wheat bread
4 T. Thousand Island salad
   dressing
2 slices bacon, crisply cooked
   and crumbled
1 c. lettuce, shredded

1/2 c. tomato, diced
2 t. carrot, peeled and diced
1 t. fresh Italian parsley, minced
1 t. fine sea salt
1/4 t. pepper

Spread each slice of bread on one side with one tablespoon salad dressing; set aside. Combine remaining ingredients in a bowl; mix well. Spoon 1/4 cup of mixture onto 2 bread slices; top with remaining bread and press down. Cut into halves or quarters. Makes 2 sandwiches.

Toasted Tomato Sandwich

Wendy Ball
Battle Creek, MI

My grandfather grew the biggest, best, juiciest tomatoes ever. He introduced me to this sandwich, the simplest way to enjoy them besides eating right from the garden. Each time I slice a wondrous hand-filling tomato and place it between toasted bread, it brings back the best memories of Grandfather working in his garden and eating the fruits of his labor.

2 slices sourdough, ciabatta or
   white bread, toasted
mayonnaise to taste
1 large heirloom, beefsteak or
   Big Boy tomato, sliced

Optional: 1 slice sweet onion
salt and pepper to taste

Spread toasted bread on one side with mayonnaise. Top one slice with tomato and onion, if desired. Season with salt and pepper; top with remaining toast slice and serve. Makes one sandwich.

Simple
Party Foods
to Share

FRESH FARMHOUSE
Recipes

Fresh-Picked Garden Salsa

Lauren Duddy
Wilmington, DE

This is a homemade salsa recipe that I created one summer with all the fresh veggies from my garden. It works best with several types of tomatoes...heirloom, roma or whatever you have planted. You can use more or less of each ingredient, depending on your preference. I like to serve it with tortilla chips at barbecues.

2 ears sweet corn
6 ripe tomatoes, chopped
2 green peppers, chopped
1 red pepper, chopped
1 red onion, chopped

1 jalapeño pepper, chopped and
   seeds removed, if desired
1 T. fresh cilantro, chopped, or
   1 t. dried cilantro
salt and pepper to taste

Steam or boil corn until tender; cut off kernels. Add kernels and remaining ingredients to a large bowl and mix well. Serve immediately, or cover and refrigerate for 2 to 4 hours to allow flavors to develop. Keeps well when refrigerated for up to 2 days. Serves 6 to 8.

Add extra texture to fresh veggies for dipping! Use a crinkle cutter or a spiral slicer to cut them into slices and sticks.

Simple Party Foods to Share

White Queso Spinach Dip

Ann Farris
Biscoe, AR

I wanted a cheese dip that was a little different, so I came up with this recipe...it's yummy and can be served right in the skillet. Serve with corn chips.

1 T. canola oil
2 c. fresh baby spinach
1 T. butter
2 T. all-purpose flour
3/4 c. whole milk
1/2 t. garlic powder

8-oz. pkg. white American
 cheese, chopped
8-oz. pkg. shredded Monterey
 Jack cheese
Optional: pico de gallo salsa,
 diced avocado

Heat oil in a cast-iron skillet over medium-high heat. Add spinach; cook until just wilted and remove from skillet. Melt butter in same skillet. Sprinkle with flour; cook and stir for 20 seconds. Gradually stir in milk; add garlic powder and whisk well. Add cheeses; cook and stir for one to 2 minutes, until thick and bubbly. Stir in wilted spinach. Place skillet under the broiler. Broil for one to 2 minutes, until golden on top. Garnish with salsa and avocado, if desired. Serves 10.

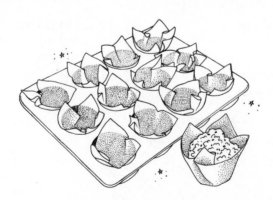

Serve a favorite yummy hot or cold dip spooned into crisp wonton cups...so easy, yet so impressive on an appetizer tray! Coat a muffin tin with non-stick vegetable spray, then press a wonton wrapper gently into each cup. Spray again and bake at 350 degrees for 8 minutes, or until golden. Fill as desired.

FRESH FARMHOUSE
Recipes

Sweet & Spicy Chicken Bacon Wraps

Lisa Robason
Corpus Christi, TX

This is a quick & easy appetizer...great for gatherings anytime!
Wonderful served with this cool, homemade Buttermilk Ranch Dip.

1-1/4 lbs. boneless, skinless, chicken breasts, cut into 1-inch cubes
1 lb. bacon, slices cut into thirds

2/3 c. brown sugar, packed
2 T. chili powder
1/2 t. pepper
1/8 t. cayenne pepper, or to taste

Make Buttermilk Ranch Dip ahead of time; refrigerate. Wrap each chicken cube in a piece of bacon. Secure with wooden toothpicks; set aside. In a shallow bowl, stir together brown sugar and seasonings. Coat chicken cubes in mixture. Spray a wire rack and a broiler pan with non-stick vegetable spray. Arrange chicken cubes on rack in broiler pan. Bake, uncovered, at 350 degrees for 30 to 35 minutes, until bacon is crisp and chicken juices run clear, turning once. Serve with ranch dip. Serves 6 to 8.

Buttermilk Ranch Dip:

1-3/4 c. sour cream
1/4 c. buttermilk
1 t. dried parsley
1/2 t. garlic powder
1/4 t. onion powder

1/8 t. dried thyme
1/8 t. dried dill weed
3/4 t. seasoned salt
1/2 t. pepper

Mix together all ingredients. Cover and refrigerate several hours before serving, to allow flavors to develop. Makes 2 cups.

If you tickle the earth with a hoe,
she laughs with a harvest.
–Douglas Jerrold

Simple Party Foods to Share

Maple Bacon & Cheddar Jalapeños

Caroline Timbs
Cord, AR

These appetizers are everyone's favorite during summer cook-outs and celebrations. We grow our own jalapeños to use for them. We often grill dozens at a time on a rack on our gas grill.

8-oz. pkg. cream cheese, softened
1 c. shredded Cheddar cheese
1 T. brown sugar, packed

16 jalapeño peppers, halved lengthwise and seeded
1 lb. maple bacon, slices cut in half

In a bowl, blend cheeses and brown sugar. Spoon one teaspoon of cheese mixture into each pepper half; wrap with bacon and place on a grilling plate. Grill on low grill setting for about 30 minutes, until bacon is crisp and golden. May also place peppers on a baking sheet; bake at 350 degrees for 30 minutes. Makes about 2-1/2 dozen.

3-2-1 Bruschetta

Cyndy DeStefano
Hermitage, PA

When tomatoes are in season, this bruschetta is a regular at our home. Many nights we'll have this with a salad for our dinner. Quick, easy and delicious! Three spoonfuls of one ingredient, one spoonful of two others...and it's ready to eat! The topping is also tasty spooned over pasta or chicken.

7 plum tomatoes, chopped
3 T. olive oil
1 T. garlic, minced

1 T. balsamic vinegar
crusty bread or garlic bread slices

Mix together all ingredients except bread. Let stand for 30 minutes, to allow flavors to blend. To serve, spoon onto slices of crusty bread or garlic bread. Serves 6.

FRESH FARMHOUSE
Recipes

Warm Ranch Chicken Dip

Beckie Apple
Grannis, AR

I am always experimenting with new recipes or putting my own spin on old ones. This appetizer is wonderful served with warm or toasted flour tortillas.

3 to 4 boneless, skinless
    chicken breasts
1/4 c. onion, diced
3 T. ranch salad dressing mix
8-oz. pkg. cream cheese,
    softened

1/2 c. real bacon bits
1-1/2 c. shredded Cheddar
    cheese
salt and pepper to taste

Arrange chicken breasts in a 4-quart slow cooker. Sprinkle with onion and ranch dressing mix; place cream cheese on top. Cover and cook on high setting for 4 to 6 hours, until chicken is very tender. Using 2 forks, shred chicken in slow cooker. Add bacon bits and shredded cheese; stir until cheese is melted. Season with salt and pepper. Serve warm. Serves 6.

Easiest-ever sandwiches for a get-together…a big platter of cold cuts, a basket of fresh breads and a choice of condiments so guests can make their own. Add some homemade potato salad plus cookies for dessert…done!

Corn & Black Bean Salsa

Laura Fank
Pella, IA

This salsa is a wonderful way to use an abundance of ripe tomatoes and peppers from the garden. It tastes like summer in a bowl...there is rarely any left over! It is great, not only with chips, but also outstanding tossed in a salad or even served as a side on its own.

15-1/2 oz. can black beans,
    drained and well rinsed
4 roma tomatoes, seeded and
    finely diced
2 to 3 jalapeño peppers, seeded
    and finely diced
1 c. corn, blanched, or thawed
    if frozen

1/2 red onion, finely diced
3 cloves garlic, finely diced
fresh cilantro to taste
coarse sea salt and cracked
    pepper to taste

Combine all ingredients in a large bowl; mix well. Serve within a day, or the onion taste will become too strong. Serves 10 to 12.

Keep creamy dips chilled in a vintage pie plate filled with crushed ice. Nestle a bowl into the ice to keep the dip chilled...country style!

FRESH FARMHOUSE
Recipes

Bacon Balls with Dill Dip

Lynda Hart
Bluffdale, UT

Delicious little morsels with a special dip!

2 c. biscuit baking mix
1/2 lb. bacon, crisply cooked
   and crumbled
3 T. green pepper, finely minced

2/3 c. milk
1/8 t. pepper
2 T. onion soup mix
1 egg, beaten

In a large bowl, mix together all ingredients except egg. Shape dough into walnut-size balls, or roll out dough 1/4-inch thick on a floured surface and cut out with a 2" round cookie cutter. Arrange on ungreased baking sheets; brush each with beaten egg. Bake at 450 degrees for 8 to 10 minutes, until golden. Serve warm or cooled with Dill Dip. Makes about 2 dozen.

Dill Dip:

1 c. sour cream
1 t. dried dill weed

2 T. onion soup mix

Mix all ingredients well; cover and chill.

Knot the ends of picnic tablecloths and tuck them under
to keep them from blowing in the breeze.

Simple Party Foods to Share

Fried Green Beans

Linda Belon
Wintersville, OH

A crunchy, tasty treat you'll love.

1/2 lb. fresh green beans,
  trimmed
1 egg, beaten
1 c. milk
1 c. seasoned dry bread crumbs

2 t. ground cumin
1 c. all-purpose flour
oil for frying
Garnish: ranch salad dressing

Add beans to a saucepan of boiling water; boil for 5 minutes. Drain; rinse and pat dry. Whisk together egg and milk in a bowl; mix bread crumbs and cumin in a separate bowl. Place flour in a third bowl. In a skillet, heat one inch oil to 350 degrees over medium-high heat. Coat beans with flour; dip into egg mixture, then into crumb mixture. Fry beans until golden; drain on paper towels. Serve warm with ranch dressing. Serves 4.

Sausage Taco Balls

Janis Purnell
Littlestown, PA

Our most popular tailgate treat! They're great for game-day get-togethers. I even make double and triple batches to be sure there are enough to go around.

1 lb. mild or medium ground
  pork sausage
8-oz. pkg. cream cheese,
  softened

1-1/4 oz. pkg. taco seasoning
  mix
1-1/4 c. biscuit baking mix
1 c. shredded Cheddar cheese

Add all ingredients to a large bowl. With your hands or a heavy-duty stand mixer with a dough hook, mix until well combined. Roll into one-inch balls; place one inch apart on ungreased rimmed baking sheets. Bake at 400 degrees for 20 to 25 minutes, until golden. Makes about 4 dozen.

FRESH FARMHOUSE
Recipes

Hot Artichoke & Kale Dip

Marian Buckley
Fontana, CA

A delicious, healthy version of our old favorite, spinach & artichoke dip. Serve with multi-grain tortilla chips and baby carrots.

1-1/2 T. butter
1/2 c. yellow onion, diced
1 clove garlic, minced
2 c. fresh baby kale, chopped
3/4 c. marinated artichoke
    hearts, drained and diced
1/2 c. low-fat sour cream

1/2 c. low-fat cream cheese,
    softened
1/4 c. shredded Parmesan cheese
1/3 c. shredded Cheddar cheese
salt and pepper to taste
2 to 3 T. half-and-half

Melt butter in a skillet over medium heat. Sauté onion for 5 minutes, or until softened. Stir in garlic and cook for 2 minutes. Stir in kale and cook until wilted. Add artichokes, sour cream and cheeses; season with salt and pepper. Cook and stir over low heat until well blended. Stir in half-and-half to desired consistency. Transfer mixture to a lightly greased 1-1/2 quart casserole dish. Bake, uncovered, at 350 degrees for 15 to 20 minutes, until hot and bubbly. Serves 4.

Slice a stack of kale into salad ribbons in a jiffy. Stack several leaves together and roll them up lengthwise, then slice thinly across the roll with a sharp knife.

158

Simple Party Foods to Share

Warm Broccoli & Cheddar Dip *Kathy Grashoff*
Fort Wayne, IN

A hot dip is always a warm welcome when the air turns chilly! Serve with crackers, party bread or pita chips.

16-oz. container sour cream
10-oz. pkg. frozen chopped
  broccoli, thawed and
  patted dry

1.4-oz. pkg. vegetable soup mix
1 c. shredded Cheddar cheese,
  divided
Optional: 1/2 t. cayenne pepper

In a large bowl, combine sour cream, broccoli, soup mix, 1/4 cup Cheddar cheese and cayenne pepper, if using. Mix well. Transfer to a lightly greased one-quart casserole dish. Bake, uncovered, at 350 degrees for 30 minutes. Top with remaining cheese; let stand until cheese melts. Serve warm. Makes 6 to 8 servings.

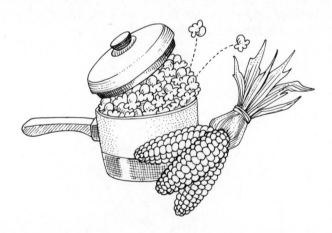

In the Midwest, you can find farmers who sell homegrown popcorn at the market! To remove the kernels, hold an ear firmly in both hands and twist until the kernels drop off. Pop kernels the old-fashioned way, on the stove, or in a microwave popcorn popper.

FRESH FARMHOUSE
Recipes

Antipasto Loaf

Sarah Oravecz
Gooseberry Patch

*This packable party sandwich goes together in
no time at all! We love all its fresh flavors.*

12-oz. French bread baguette,
   halved lengthwise
8-oz. container spreadable
   cream cheese
3 T. jarred pesto sauce
2 c. baby spinach, coarsely
   chopped

1/2 c. sun-dried tomatoes in oil,
   drained and chopped
1/2 c. marinated artichoke
   hearts, drained and chopped
2 T. shredded Parmesan cheese

Hollow out baguette halves by pulling out the soft bread inside; set
aside. In a bowl, blend cream cheese and pesto; spread evenly into
baguette halves. Divide remaining ingredients between baguette halves.
Place halves cut-sides together; wrap tightly in plastic wrap. Refrigerate
at least one hour or up to 4 hours. Cut into slices; fasten with toothpicks,
if desired. Makes 12 servings, 2 slices each.

Try making your own pesto...it's so fresh and flavorful! Toss
together one bunch finely chopped fresh basil, 3 cloves minced
garlic, 3/4 cup freshly grated Parmesan cheese and 3 tablespoons
pine nuts. Drizzle with 3 tablespoons olive oil and stir to blend.

Simple Party Foods to Share

Arizona Dip

Donna Reeter
Vandalia, IL

Back in the mid 1970s, my parents wintered in Arizona. Mother tried a dip recipe that was printed on the back of a potato chip bag. She didn't remember the name of the chips and just called it Arizona Dip. It was a hit with family & friends! My children loved it as well...now my grandchildren request it too.

8-oz. pkg. cream cheese, room temperature
1/3 c. French or Catalina salad dressing
2 T. catsup

1 T. onion, grated, or to taste
1/8 t. salt
corn chips, pretzels or carrot and celery sticks

In a bowl, combine cream cheese, salad dressing, catsup, onion and salt; blend well. Beat until smooth; cover and chill. Serve with corn chips, pretzels or vegetable sticks. Makes 4 to 6 servings.

Ricotta-Herb Bruschetta

Amelia Smulski
Lyons, IL

A simple, easy appetizer you will turn to again & again. Feel free to substitute parsley for dill.

2 c. ricotta cheese
3 T. green onions, minced
2 T. fresh dill, minced
1 T. fresh chives, minced
1 shallot, finely minced

kosher salt and pepper to taste
1 round loaf sourdough bread, thinly sliced
olive oil to taste

In a small bowl, stir together all ingredients except bread and olive oil. Cover and chill. At serving time, toast bread as desired. Spoon mixture onto toast slices; drizzle lightly with olive oil and serve. Serves 6.

FRESH FARMHOUSE
Recipes

Stuffed Mini Peppers

Linda Peterson
Mason, MI

This is my go-to recipe when I want a healthy appetizer. Ground turkey or beef can be used as well. The mini sweet peppers come in packages of assorted colors, which look so pretty on a platter.

1-1/2 lbs. ground chicken
2 t. onion powder
1 t. chili powder
1/2 t. ground cumin
1/2 t. garlic powder
1/2 t. smoked paprika
1 t. salt
1/2 t. cornstarch
1/2 c. water
1 c. corn, thawed if frozen

1 c. black beans, drained
  and rinsed
2 lbs. mini sweet peppers,
  halved lengthwise and seeds
  removed
1 c. shredded Mexican-blend
  cheese
Garnish: sour cream, sliced green
  onions and black olives

In a large skillet, cook chicken over medium-high heat until browned and cooked through. Stir in seasonings, cornstarch and water. Cook over medium heat an additional 5 minutes, stirring occasionally, until thickened. Stir in corn and beans. Arrange pepper halves on a lightly greased baking sheet. Spoon one to 2 tablespoons chicken mixture into each. Bake at 350 degrees for 15 minutes, or until peppers are soft. Remove from oven; sprinkle shredded cheese over peppers. Return to oven for 2 to 3 minutes, until cheese is melted. Garnish as desired. Serves 8.

Tuck simple bouquets of black-eyed susans, zinnias, daisies and other cut flowers into empty tin cans with bright-colored veggie labels. Line them up down the center of a party table...charming!

Simple Party Foods to Share

Beer-Battered Zucchini

Rita Morgan
Pueblo, CO

My family loves this scrumptious alternative to French fries! We've even been known to make it over a campfire on camping trips.

1-1/2 c. all-purpose flour
1 t. baking powder
1/2 t. salt, divided
7-oz. bottle regular or
    non-alcoholic beer
1 egg, beaten
2 zucchini, quartered lengthwise
    and cut into 4-inch pieces

2 t. seafood seasoning
1 t. ground cumin
oil for deep-frying
1/2 c. ranch or honey mustard
    salad dressing
Garnish: lemon wedges

In a bowl, combine flour, baking powder and 1/4 teaspoon salt; whisk in beer and egg until smooth. Let batter stand 15 minutes. In another bowl, toss zucchini pieces with seafood seasoning and cumin. Add zucchini to batter and toss to coat. Remove, letting excess batter drip off. In a skillet, heat one inch oil over medium-high heat to 350 degrees. Add zucchini in batches, cooking and turning once until tender and golden. Drain on paper towels; sprinkle with remaining salt. Serve warm with salad dressing and lemon wedges. Serves 4.

Choosing an oil for deep frying? With a mild flavor and a high smoke point, canola oil is excellent. It's economical too.

FRESH FARMHOUSE
Recipes

Fruit Salsa & Cinnamon Crisps
Angela Evans
Brookneal, VA

*Everyone loves this sweet salsa at parties or for snacking...
even at brunch! Mix & match berries as you like.*

2 Golden Delicious apples,
  peeled and diced
1 lb. strawberries, hulled
  and diced
3/4 lb. fresh raspberries or
  blueberries
2 kiwi, peeled and diced

3 T. raspberry or strawberry
  preserves
1 T. brown sugar, packed
5 T. sugar, divided
6 10-inch flour tortillas
1 T. cinnamon

In a large bowl, gently mix together fruits, preserves, brown sugar and
2 tablespoons sugar. Cover and chill. Meanwhile, to make cinnamon
crisps, spray tortillas on both sides with butter-flavored non-stick
vegetable spray. Cut into wedges or wide strips with a pizza cutter.
Arrange in a single layer on ungreased baking sheets. Combine
cinnamon and remaining sugar; sprinkle over tortillas. Spray lightly
with butter spray again. Bake at 350 degrees for 8 to 10 minutes, until
crisp. Serve warm crisps with fruit salsa. Makes 10 servings.

Create a warm party glow in a jiffy, using box graters
picked up at flea markets. Simply tuck a votive or
tealight inside...so simple!

Simple Party Foods to Share

Balsamic Plum Preserves Appetizer

April Garner
Independence, KY

This makes a great quick & easy appetizer! Just spoon over a block of cream cheese and serve with your favorite cracker or bagel crisps.

4-1/2 c. ripe plums, halved,
    pitted and chopped
1-1/2 c. sugar
3 T. balsamic vinegar

1-3/4 oz. pkg. powdered fruit
    pectin
1 T. fresh basil, chopped
8-oz. pkg. cream cheese

In a microwave-safe glass bowl, stir together plums, sugar, vinegar and pectin. Microwave on high for 8 minutes; mixture will boil. Stir; microwave on high another 8 to 10 minutes, until thickened, resembling pancake syrup. Stir in basil. Cool mixture completely, about 2 hours. Serve spooned over cream cheese on a serving plate, or cover and chill preserves in an airtight container. Store in refrigerator up to 3 weeks. Makes 10 servings.

Honeydew Cooler

Jo Ann
Gooseberry Patch

We love this refreshing beverage! For another delicious way, replace some of the melon with cubed, seeded cucumber.

8 c. honeydew melon, cut into
    1/2-inch cubes, divided
6-oz. can frozen lemonade
    concentrate, divided

1/3 c. water
1-1/2 c. ginger ale, chilled

Place melon cubes in a single layer on a large baking sheet; freeze for 8 hours. Shortly before serving time, let stand at room temperature for 15 minutes. In a blender, combine half each of melon cubes and lemonade concentrate. Process until smooth and pour into a pitcher; repeat with remaining melon and concentrate. Add water and ginger ale; stir gently and serve. Makes 8 servings.

FRESH FARMHOUSE
Recipes

Herb Garden Cheese Ball

*Liz Plotnick-Snay
Gooseberry Patch*

*Easy to double! To use fresh herbs, simply measure 2 teaspoons
of each herb. Serve with assorted crackers.*

8-oz. pkg. cream cheese,
   softened
1 clove garlic, pressed
1 t. dried basil

1 t. dill weed
1 t. dried chives
1 t. caraway seed
Garnish: lemon pepper seasoning

Combine all ingredients except garnish in a food processor or a bowl.
Process or blend until well mixed. Form into a ball or log; roll lightly in
lemon pepper to coat. Wrap well in plastic wrap; refrigerate overnight to
blend flavors. Makes one cup.

Dilly of a Dip

*Julie Ann Perkins
Anderson, IN*

*Want a scrumptious way to show off those garden goodies? Enhance
their flavors with this dilly of a dip! Serve with celery and carrot
sticks, sweet peppers, cucumbers and cherry tomatoes.*

1 c. mayonnaise
1 c. sour cream
2 T. fresh parsley, snipped

2 to 3 T. fresh dill weed, snipped
2 t. seasoned salt

Blend all ingredients together. Cover and chill for several hours to allow
the flavors to come together. Makes 2 cups.

Snap up stoneware butter crocks when
you find them at flea markets. They're
just the right size for serving party
spreads and dips as well as butter.

Simple Party Foods to Share

Stuffed Spring Peas

Paula Marchesi
Auburn, PA

Here's an easy recipe for all your get-togethers. Pretty on a platter...finger food made simple! I love spring peas and surround them with fresh strawberries.

8-oz. container spreadable garlic
   & herb cream cheese
1/2 t. dill weed

1/2 t. caraway seed
36 fresh snow peas, trimmed

In a large bowl, blend cream cheese, dill weed and caraway seed. Cover and refrigerate for 3 hours or overnight. Let stand at room temperature for at least 30 minutes. Meanwhile, bring a large saucepan of water to a boil. Add snow peas; cover and boil for one to 2 minutes. Drain; immediately add peas to ice water. Drain; pat dry. Gently split pea pods open. Pipe or spoon one teaspoon of filling into each pea pod. Arrange on a platter; chill up to 2 hours, until serving time. Makes 3 dozen.

Blue Cheese-Stuffed Tomatoes

Kim Kopet
Hampstead, NH

These tasty little delights are always the first to go at all my dinner parties!

24 cherry tomatoes
3 3-oz. pkgs. cream cheese,
   softened
1/4 c. crumbled blue cheese

1 T. fresh chives, chopped
1 T. lemon juice
2 drops hot pepper sauce

Gently cut tops off tomatoes. Scoop out seeds and pulp; discard. Place tomatoes upside-down on a paper towel to drain. In a bowl, blend remaining ingredients until smooth. Spoon mixture into tomatoes; serve immediately, or cover and chill. Makes 2 dozen.

For stand-up parties, make it easy on guests by serving foods that can be eaten in one or 2 bites.

FRESH FARMHOUSE
Recipes

Super Sunday Caviar

Anne Alesauskas
Minocqua, WI

This is one of my favorite fresh foods of all time! I love to gather lots of ingredients from the farmers' market and mix them up to see what happens. I have also added red onion, Cheddar cheese or bean and corn salsa to this recipe. Serve with corn or tortilla chips, or spoon onto fresh-grilled burgers. Delicious!

2 16-oz. cans black-eyed peas, drained
15-1/2 oz. can white or yellow hominy, drained
14-1/2 oz. can diced tomatoes with garlic
4-oz. can chopped green chiles
3.8-oz. can sliced black olives, drained
2 avocados, peeled, pitted and chopped

1 bunch green onions, chopped
1/2 c. crumbled feta cheese
1/4 c. garlic, minced
2 T. extra-virgin olive oil
juice of 1/2 lime
1 T. sugar
1 T. ground cumin, or to taste
2 T. salt, or to taste
1 T. pepper, or to taste

Combine all ingredients together in a large bowl; mix well. Cover and refrigerate for at least one hour. Makes 10 to 12 servings.

If you're short on table space, an old-fashioned wooden ironing board makes a sturdy sideboard. Just adjust it to a convenient height, add a pretty table runner and set out the food...come & get it!

Simple Party Foods to Share

Best Strawberry-Lemonade Punch

Michelle Powell
Valley, AL

This is the best punch! It's a favorite for our church showers and summer suppers. Very easy and inexpensive to make.

2 46-oz. cans unsweetened
    pineapple juice
8 c. cold water
6 c. sugar, or to taste
3 envs. unsweetened strawberry
    drink mix

3 envs. unsweetened lemonade
    drink mix
8-oz. can crushed pineapple
2 ltrs. ginger ale, chilled

In a large plastic freezer container, combine pineapple juice, water, sugar and drink mixes. Stir until sugar is dissolved. Cover and freeze. To serve, remove from freezer one to 2 hours before serving time. When thawed, pour into a punch bowl. Add pineapple and ginger ale; stir gently and serve immediately. Makes about 7-1/2 quarts.

Pick up a dozen pint-size Mason jars. They're perfect for serving cold beverages at casual get-togethers.

FRESH FARMHOUSE
Recipes

Succulent Stuffed Mushrooms

Janis Parr
Ontario, Canada

This is a scrumptious hot appetizer full of flavor and texture that everyone loves. I've made these so many times, as they're always requested when we get together with friends.

12 medium Portabella
  mushrooms
1/4 c. butter, divided
1/2 c. green onions, finely
  chopped
1/3 c. water chestnuts,
  finely chopped

1/2 t. Worcestershire sauce
1/2 t. soy sauce
1/8 t. pepper
1/4 c. unseasoned dry bread
  crumbs
1/4 t. salt

Remove stems from mushrooms; set aside mushroom caps. Finely chop stems. In a skillet, melt 2 tablespoons butter over medium heat. Add mushroom stems, onions and water chestnuts. Cook for 6 minutes, stirring often. Stir in sauces and pepper. Remove from heat; stir in bread crumbs. Fill each mushroom cap with one tablespoon filling. Place filled caps in a greased 13"x9" baking pan. Melt remaining butter; brush onto mushrooms. Lightly sprinkle with salt. Bake, uncovered, at 425 degrees for 12 to 15 minutes, until lightly golden. Serve warm. Serves 6 to 8.

Homemade buttermilk dressing is wonderful on salads... a kid-friendly dip for veggies too! Blend 1/2 cup buttermilk, 1/2 cup mayonnaise, one teaspoon dried parsley, 1/2 teaspoon onion powder, 1/4 teaspoon garlic powder, 1/8 teaspoon dill weed and a little salt and pepper. Keep refrigerated.

Simple Party Foods to Share

Jalapeño Popper Dip

Toni Groves
Benld, IL

Everyone likes this dip! We serve it at all of our family gatherings, and we usually make at least a double batch. Serve with assorted crackers.

8-oz. pkg. cream cheese, softened
1 c. sour cream
1 t. garlic powder
8-oz. pkg. shredded Cheddar cheese

3/4 c. shredded Parmesan cheese, divided
4-oz. can diced jalapeño peppers, well drained

Combine cream cheese, sour cream and garlic powder in a large bowl. Beat with an electric mixer on medium speed until fluffy. Add cheeses and jalapeños; mix well. Spread in a lightly greased 8"x8" baking pan; sprinkle with Crumb Topping. Bake, uncovered, at 375 degrees for 15 to 20 minutes, until bubbly and golden. Makes 6 servings.

Crumb Topping:

1 c. panko bread crumbs
1/4 c. shredded Parmesan cheese

1/4 c. butter, melted
1 T. fresh parsley, chopped

Combine all ingredients; mix well.

Fresh jalapeño peppers are extra flavorful, but take care when slicing them. It's best to wear plastic gloves, and be sure not to touch your eyes!

FRESH FARMHOUSE
Recipes

Mick's Off-the-Beaten-Trail Mix *Marta Norton*
Redlands, CA

*This stuff is addictively good and easily adapted to your tastes.
I use all shelled and roasted salted nuts and seeds. Sometimes I'll
add some chocolate chips or candy-coated chocolates...yummy!*

1 lb. cashew pieces
1 lb. peanuts
1 lb. golden raisins
1 lb. raisins
1 lb. pumpkin seeds
1 lb. pepitas

1 lb. sunflower seeds
1/2 lb. pistachio nuts
1/2 lb. pine nuts
1/2 lb. sweetened, dried
 cranberries

Mix together all ingredients in a very large container. Store in tightly
sealed containers. Makes 8-1/2 pounds, or 2 one-gallon plastic
zipping bags.

Fill an old wooden bucket with crushed ice and bottles of
soda pop for a real farmhouse feel. Everyone can help
themselves to a favorite frosty beverage!

Simple Party Foods to Share

Refreshing Rhubarb Slush

Debbie Joramo
Sleepy Eye, MN

A perfect beverage for summertime parties and wedding showers.

12 c. rhubarb, chopped
9 c. water
2 c. sugar
12-oz. can frozen orange
   juice concentrate

12-oz. can frozen lemonade
   concentrate
3-oz. pkg. strawberry or
   raspberry gelatin mix
2 ltrs. lemon-line soda, chilled

In a stockpot over medium heat, simmer rhubarb, water and sugar for 30 minutes, stirring until sugar dissolves. Strain well, discarding solids; transfer to a large ice cream pail. Add frozen concentrates and gelatin mix; stir well. Cover and freeze. To serve, partially thaw mixture until slushy. Fill punch cups with half slush, half chilled soda; serve immediately. Makes 20 to 25 servings.

Raspberry Iced Tea Cooler

Megan Lowe
Dover, DE

Deliciously different from plain old iced tea!

16 c. water
1-1/2 c. sugar
4 family-size tea bags

12-oz. pkg. frozen unsweetened
   raspberries, thawed
1/4 c. lemon juice

In a stockpot over medium heat, bring water to a boil. Remove from heat. Add sugar and stir until dissolved. Add remaining ingredients; stir well. Cover and let stand for 5 minutes. Strain, discarding solids and tea bags. Pour into a large pitcher and chill thoroughly. Makes 18 to 20 servings.

Plant a seed of friendship;
reap a bouquet of happiness.
—Lois L. Kaufman

FRESH FARMHOUSE
Recipes

Braunschweiger Spread

Barbara Klein
Newburgh, IN

I love to make this hearty spread for holiday parties. Serve with regular or buttery whole-wheat crackers or shredded wheat crackers. Guests will love it!

8-oz. pkg. braunschweiger
8-oz. pkg. cream cheese,
   softened and divided
2 t. dill pickle juice
1 t. Worcestershire sauce
3 drops hot pepper sauce

1/4 t. garlic salt
1/4 c. butter, softened
1/4 c. onion, chopped
1/3 c. dill pickle chips, drained
   and chopped
1/2 c. chopped pecans

In a large bowl, mash braunschweiger with a fork. Add half of cream cheese, pickle juice, sauces and garlic salt. Beat thoroughly with an electric mixer on medium speed until blended. Mix in butter, onion and pickles. Pack mixture into an aluminum foil-lined bowl; cover and refrigerate for 2 hours. To serve, turn out on a plate; remove foil. Spread remaining cream cheese over ball and coat with pecans. Serves 10.

Vintage cutting boards in fun shapes are perfect for serving up a variety of cheeses and other finger foods.

Simple Party Foods to Share

Savory Cheese & Sausage Bites

Virginia Campbell
Clifton Forge, VA

One of my most popular appetizers ever! A great icebreaker and conversation-starter because everyone gathers around the table. Use hot, maple or sage-flavored sausage for extra flavor.

2 lbs. ground pork sausage
1-1/2 c. biscuit baking mix
2 8-oz. pkgs. shredded sharp or
    extra-sharp Cheddar cheese
1/2 c. onion, finely chopped
1/2 c. celery, finely chopped

1 t. garlic salt
1/2 t. coarse pepper
1/4 t. red pepper flakes
Optional: honey mustard, ranch
    salad dressing or chili sauce

Combine all ingredients except optional sauces in a large bowl. Using your hands, mix well and form into one-inch balls. Place on ungreased baking sheets. Bake at 375 degrees for 18 to 20 minutes, until golden. Remove from oven; cool for 5 minutes before removing from pan. If desired, serve with a variety of dips. Serves 10 to 12.

Savor warm, sunny days outdoors. Pull together mismatched yard sale finds, or spruce up the lawn chairs you have... it's easy! Spray paint them all the same color, or use a rainbow of colors just for fun.

FRESH FARMHOUSE
Recipes

Roasted Onion Dip

Karen Wilson
Defiance, OH

This delicious dip can be made ahead and baked when your guests arrive. Serve with tortilla chips or crackers.

3 sweet onions, peeled
2 T. olive oil
2 8-oz. pkgs. cream cheese,
  softened
8-oz. pkg. shredded mozzarella
  cheese

1-1/4 c. shredded Swiss cheese
1/2 c. mayonnaise
Garnish: chopped fresh parsley
tortilla chips or snack crackers

Place onions on an aluminum foil-lined baking sheet; drizzle with olive oil. Bake at 400 degrees for 35 to 40 minutes, until onions are tender and golden. Let onions cool on pan for 15 minutes. Meanwhile, in a bowl, combine cheeses and mayonnaise; mix until smooth. Chop cooled onions; mix into cheese mixture. Spoon mixture into a lightly greased 2-quart casserole dish. Bake, uncovered, at 400 degrees for 30 to 40 minutes, until hot and bubbly. Garnish with parsley; serve warm with tortilla chips or crackers. Serves 8.

Invite guests into your backyard for an evening cookout.
Hang lanterns on the fence and in the trees for
twinkling light...magical!

Simple Party Foods to Share

Granny's Cheese Straws

Kayla Herring
Hartwell, GA

My Grandmother Betty often catered weddings or other events. These cheese straws were sure to be on the menu!

2 8-oz. pkgs. shredded sharp
   Cheddar cheese
1/2 c. butter
2 c. all-purpose flour
1 t. baking powder
1 t. salt
1 t. sugar

In a large bowl, blend cheese and butter; set aside. Sift remaining ingredients into another bowl; add to cheese mixture and mix well. Knead dough until smooth. On a floured surface, roll out small portions of dough at a time, 1/2 inch thick. Cut into strips, 1/4 inch wide and one inch long. Dough may also be rolled into one-inch balls and flattened with a fork. Place on parchment paper-lined baking sheets. Bake at 350 degrees for 12 to 16 minutes, until lightly golden. Makes about 3 dozen.

Chunky Salsa Dip

Christi Vawter
Sheridan, IN

Wherever I take this dip, it's the star of the show! I always end up sharing the recipe, which was passed to me by my sixth-grade teacher, Mrs. Weaver. It's also tasty spooned onto tacos, burgers and grilled chicken.

1 lb. mild Cheddar cheese,
   coarsely shredded
2 avocados, peeled, pitted
   and diced
12 roma tomatoes, diced
2 bunches green onions, diced
32-oz. jar salsa verde
tortilla chips

Add cheese and vegetables to a very large bowl; do not stir. Cover and refrigerate until ready to serve. At serving time, pour salsa over all. Stir very gently, just enough to combine ingredients. Serve with tortilla chips. Makes 24 servings.

FRESH FARMHOUSE
Recipes

Cheesy Spinach Bread

Judy Henfey
Cibolo, TX

*This is an easy appetizer to prepare for Christmas dinner
or other get-togethers. It always gets thumbs-up and
people ask for the recipe...delicious!*

10-oz. pkg. frozen chopped
   spinach
1/2 c. onion, chopped
1/2 c. butter
4-oz. can sliced mushrooms,
   drained and chopped
1 c. shredded Cheddar cheese

1 c. shredded mozzarella cheese
hot pepper sauce to taste
salt and pepper to taste
1 loaf French bread, halved
   lengthwise
1/2 c. grated Parmesan cheese

Cook spinach according to package instructions; drain very well.
Meanwhile, combine onion and butter in a microwave-safe bowl.
Microwave on high for 2 to 3 minutes, until onion is tender. In a large
bowl, combine spinach, onion mixture, mushrooms, Cheddar and
mozzarella cheeses, hot sauce, salt and pepper; mix well. Spread
mixture on cut sides of both halves of loaf. Place on an ungreased
baking sheet; sprinkle with Parmesan cheese. Bake at 350 degrees for
10 to 15 minutes, until hot and bubbly. Slice to serve. Serves 8.

Save seeds from this year's garden to plant next spring...fun to
share with friends too! Collect flowers and seed pods, then shake
out the seeds onto paper towels. When they're dry, place seeds
in small paper envelopes, label them and seal in canning jars.

Simple Party Foods to Share

Olive-Stuffed Eggs

Bev Traxler
British Columbia, Canada

These tasty eggs are always a hit at gatherings and they're easy to make. Add more olives, if you like.

6 eggs, hard-boiled, peeled and
    halved lengthwise
1/4 c. mayonnaise
2 T. mustard
1/4 t. salt
1/8 t. pepper
6 green olives with pimentos,
    chopped, or more to taste
Garnish: paprika to taste

Gently remove egg yolks and place in a bowl; arrange egg whites on a plate and set aside. Using a fork, finely crumble yolks. Add mayonnaise, mustard, salt, pepper and olives; mix well. Spoon mixture into centers of egg whites; sprinkle with paprika. Cover and refrigerate until serving time. Makes one dozen.

Everyone loves deviled eggs! If there's no deviled egg plate handy, simply line a serving plate with curly parsley or lettuce, then nestle the eggs in the greens.

FRESH FARMHOUSE
Recipes

Spicy Barbecue Chicken Wings
Eleanor Dionne
Beverly, MA

This recipe was given to me by a neighbor many years ago. The sauce is scrumptious on pork spareribs, boneless chicken tenders or just about any cut of meat you want to barbecue.

2 c. water
1 c. catsup
1/2 c. Worcestershire sauce
1 t. lemon juice

1 t. salt
3 to 4 lbs. chicken wings,
   separated

In a saucepan, combine water, catsup, Worcestershire sauce, lemon juice and salt; mix well, Simmer over medium heat for about 5 minutes. Arrange wings in a greased rimmed baking sheet; spoon sauce over wings. Bake, uncovered, at 450 degrees for 30 minutes. Drain fat from pan. Reduce heat to 350 degrees; bake for an additional 40 minutes, basting often with sauce. Serves 8.

Onion Strings
Lynda Robson
Boston, MA

Delicious! Serve with catsup or ranch dressing for dipping, or heap on grilled burgers.

1 egg, beaten
1/2 c. milk
2 sweet onions, thinly sliced

2 c. all-purpose flour
2 t. seasoning salt
oil for frying

In a small bowl, whisk together egg and milk. Put sliced onions in a large bowl; pour egg mixture over onions. Turn onions to coat thoroughly; transfer onions to a colander and drain. Combine flour and salt in a plastic zipping bag. Add onions and shake to coat. Heat 2 inches oil to 375 degrees in a deep skillet. Working in batches, add onions to hot oil and cook for just one to 2 minutes, until golden. Remove to paper towels with tongs. Makes 4 servings.

Freeze freshly washed mint leaves in an ice cube tray...
so refreshing in glasses of lemonade or ice water.

Fresh & Delicious Desserts

FRESH FARMHOUSE
Recipes

Plum Delicious Crisp

Janis Parr
Ontario, Canada

This fruity crisp is scrumptious and a big hit with everyone.
Leftovers may be warmed up, if there are any!

12 ripe plums, halved, pitted
   and sliced
1/2 c. plus 2 T. all-purpose flour,
   divided
1/2 c. sugar
1 c. brown sugar, packed
   and divided

1 T. lemon juice
1/2 c. old-fashioned oats,
   uncooked
1/2 t. cinnamon
1/2 t. nutmeg
1/3 c. butter, softened
Garnish: vanilla ice cream

In a large bowl, combine plums, 2 tablespoons flour, sugar, 1/4 cup
brown sugar and lemon juice. Toss well; spread mixture in a greased
8"x8" baking pan and set aside. In another bowl, combine remaining
flour, remaining brown sugar, oats and spices; stir to combine. Blend
in butter with a pastry blender until mixture resembles coarse crumbs.
Sprinkle crumb mixture over plum mixture. Bake at 350 degrees for
30 minutes. Serve warm, topped with ice cream. Makes 6 to 8 servings.

Nothing says farm-fresh flavor like dollops of whipped cream
on a homemade dessert. It's easy too. In a chilled bowl,
with chilled beaters, whip one cup of whipping cream
until soft peaks form. Mix in 2 teaspoons sugar and
2 teaspoons vanilla extract...and enjoy!

Fresh & Delicious Desserts

Aunt Bessie's Fresh Apple Cake
Sharon Goss
Indianapolis, IN

My dad had five sisters who were all wonderful cooks. Each sister had a specialty. Cakes and desserts were my Aunt Bessie's specialty. Without a doubt, my favorite was her Fresh Apple Cake. It was like biting into an autumn day!

2 eggs, beaten
1 c. oil
2 c. sugar
1 t. vanilla extract
2-1/2 c. self-rising flour

1 T. cinnamon
3 c. apples, peeled, cored
   and diced
1 c. chopped walnuts

In a large bowl, beat eggs, oil and sugar with an electric mixer on medium speed. Mix in vanilla; set aside. In another bowl, sift together flour and cinnamon; add to egg mixture. Fold in apples and walnuts. Divide batter between 2 greased 8"x8" baking pans. Bake at 350 degrees for about 45 minutes. May also use a 13"x9" baking pan; bake for about one hour. Cut into squares. Makes 18 servings.

Vintage teacups can be had for a song at tag sales. Start a collection with a single theme...all cups with pink roses, blue forget-me-nots or whatever strikes your fancy. Sure to be a fun topic of conversation at any tea party!

FRESH FARMHOUSE
Recipes

Streusel-Topped Carrot Cake

Jo Ann
Gooseberry Patch

Everyone loves this cake! It's filled with sweet carrots and pineapple and finished with a crunchy streusel topping. Makes enough for a crowd!

3 c. all-purpose flour
2-1/2 c. sugar
2 t. baking powder
1 t. baking soda
2 t. cinnamon
1/2 t. salt
1-1/2 c. oil

3 eggs, beaten
2 c. carrots, peeled and
  coarsely grated
8-oz. can crushed pineapple
  in syrup
1 t. vanilla extract

In a large bowl, sift together flour, sugar, baking powder, baking soda, cinnamon and salt. Add oil, eggs, carrots, pineapple with syrup and vanilla. Beat with an electric mixer on medium-high speed for about 4 minutes. Pour batter into a greased 15"x10" jelly-roll pan. Sprinkle evenly with Streusel Topping. Bake at 350 degrees for one hour, or until cake tests done when tested with a wooden pick. Cut into squares. Serves 15 to 18.

Streusel Topping:

1/2 c. all-purpose flour
1/2 c. brown sugar, packed
1 t. cinnamon

1/4 c. butter
Optional: 1/2 c. chopped nuts

Mix together flour, brown sugar and cinnamon; cut in butter until crumbly. Add nuts, if desired.

Cutting a cake with sticky frosting? Between slices, simply dip the knife in hot water and wipe it clean with a paper towel.

Fresh & Delicious Desserts

Beulah's Old-Fashioned Brownies

Pat Beach
Fisherville, KY

This recipe was given to me by a sweet elderly volunteer at a medical office where I worked years ago. Every Friday she brought in homemade goodies for the staff. We always laughed and said she was trying her best to make us gain weight. They really are delicious!

4-oz. pkg. bittersweet baking
  chocolate
1 c. butter
2 t. vanilla extract
1/4 t. salt

4 eggs, room temperature
2 c. sugar
1 c. all-purpose flour
2 c. chopped pecans

In a saucepan over low heat, melt chocolate and butter. Add vanilla and salt; stir until smooth. Set aside to cool to room temperature. In a large bowl, beat eggs with an electric mixer on medium speed until light and fluffy. Add sugar and continue beating. Add melted chocolate mixture and beat again. In a separate bowl, toss together flour and nuts; fold into batter. Pour batter into a greased 9"x9" baking pan. Bake at 350 degrees for 35 to 45 minutes. Cut into squares. Makes 8 to 10 servings.

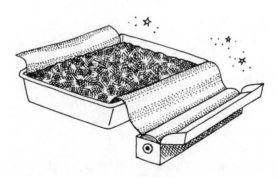

Line your brownie pan with aluminum foil...be sure to grease well. After brownies are baked and cooled, they'll lift right out, making cutting a snap. Best of all, clean-up is a breeze!

FRESH FARMHOUSE
Recipes

Shelly's Strawberry Trifle

Shelly Smith
Dana, IN

A great summer dessert!

2 qts. fresh strawberries, hulled
  and sliced
3 T. sugar
3/4 t. almond extract, divided
2 8-oz. pkgs. cream cheese,
  softened
8-oz. container sour cream

16-oz. container frozen whipped
  topping, thawed
2 c. powdered sugar
1/2 t. vanilla extract
16-oz. pkg. frozen angel food
  cake, thawed

In a large bowl, toss strawberries with sugar and 1/4 teaspoon almond extract; set aside. In another large bowl, combine cream cheese, sour cream, whipped topping, powdered sugar, vanilla and remaining almond extracts. Blend well; set aside. Tear cake into bite-sized pieces; fold into cream cheese mixture. In a large glass trifle dish, layer 1/3 each of cream cheese mixture and strawberry mixture. Repeat layering twice. Cover and chill until serving time. Serves 12.

Dress up warm fresh-baked desserts with a scoop of
ice cream! Serve them in a snap...simply scoop ice cream
ahead of time into paper muffin liners and freeze
on a baking sheet.

Fresh & Delicious Desserts

Mom's Rhubarb Bars

Paula Marchesi
Auburn, PA

I simply love rhubarb! I have five plants in my garden, which produce quite a bit for me. In early spring, I'll make these delicious bars along with jams, pies, cookies and cake using this tasty vegetable that's so good for you. I even make a few sauces and salsa from rhubarb.

1-1/2 c. all-purpose flour, divided
1/3 c. powdered sugar
1/2 c. chilled butter, cubed
1-1/2 c. sugar

2 eggs, beaten
2 c. rhubarb, diced
1/2 c. chopped pecans
1/2 c. flaked coconut

In a large bowl, combine one cup flour and powdered sugar. Cut in butter with a fork until crumbly. Pat into a lightly greased 13"x9" baking pan. Bake at 350 degrees for 13 to 15 minutes, until edges are lightly golden. In another bowl, combine sugar and remaining flour. Add eggs; stir in rhubarb, pecans and coconut. Spoon over baked crust. Bake at 350 degrees for 30 to 35 minutes, until set. Cool in pan on a wire rack; cut into bars. Makes 2 dozen.

If you love to bake, keep a small vintage coffee grinder on hand for grinding whole spices. The extra-fresh flavor of freshly ground nutmeg, cloves and cinnamon can't be beat.

FRESH FARMHOUSE
Recipes

Peaches & Cream Pie

Sherry Lamb Noble
Paragould, AR

This pie was created by my mother. It was a favorite dessert served in my parents' restaurant in the 1960s and 1970s, and it's still a family favorite. Mother always used fresh peaches, which gave it such a special flavor. Family & friends continue to request this pie at our gatherings. It brings me joy to continue Mother's tradition.

3 egg whites
1 c. sugar
24 buttery round crackers, crushed
1/2 c. chopped pecans
1/4 t. baking powder
2 to 3 c. ripe peaches, halved, pitted and sliced
sugar to taste
Garnish: whipped cream

In a deep bowl, beat egg whites with an electric mixer on medium to medium-high speed until stiff peaks form. Slowly add sugar; beat until sugar dissolves and set aside. In another bowl, mix together crushed crackers, pecans and baking powder; fold into eggs whites. Spoon mixture into a buttered 9" pie plate. Bake at 325 degrees for 30 minutes. Cool completely. Meanwhile, toss peaches with sugar as desired. Cut pie into wedges; top with sliced peaches and whipped cream. Serves 8.

Happiness being a dessert so sweet,
May life give you more than you can ever eat.
— Irish toast

Fresh & Delicious Desserts

Blueberry Shortcake Sundaes

Agnes Ward
Ontario, Canada

I always keep the ingredients for this yummy dessert on hand, so I can I make this dessert any time of year for family & friends or just to treat myself.

1/3 c. sugar
1-1/2 t. cornstarch
1/4 t. cinnamon
3 T. water

1-1/2 c. fresh blueberries
4 slices pound cake
4 scoops vanilla ice cream

In a small saucepan, combine sugar, cornstarch and cinnamon. Stir in water and blueberries until blended. Bring to a boil over high heat; cook and stir for 2 to 4 minutes, until thickened. To serve, place cake slices on 4 dessert plates. Top each with a scoop of ice cream and a drizzle of blueberry sauce. Serves 4.

Granny's Baked Custard

Tina Goodpasture
Meadowview, VA

Granny Hudson made the best baked custard. I so looked forward to getting my share of this sweet dessert! My son-in-law loves it just about as much as I do.

3 eggs
3 c. milk
6 T. sugar
1/4 t. salt

1 t. vanilla extract
1 T. butter
nutmeg to taste

Lightly beat eggs in a large bowl; set aside. In a saucepan over medium heat, combine milk, sugar and salt; heat just to boiling. Stir milk mixture slowly into beaten eggs; add vanilla. Transfer to 6 custard cups or a 9"x9" baking pan. Dot with butter; add a sprinkle of nutmeg. Bake at 325 degrees for about 30 minutes, until golden, being careful not to overbake. Serve warm or chilled. Serves 6.

Stir up a sweet dessert topping...combine a pint of sliced ripe strawberries with 1/4 cup strawberry jam and 1/4 cup orange juice. Yum!

FRESH FARMHOUSE
Recipes

Deb's Apricot & Sunflower Slice

Melissa Currie
Phoenix, AZ

My sister-in-law from Melbourne, Australia always makes these healthy snack bars for day trips or a ride in the car on the way to the beach house. Enjoy!

1 c. dried apricots, chopped
1/3 c. sunflower seeds
1 c. flaked coconut
1 c. bran flake cereal
2 c. crispy rice cereal

1/2 c. butter
1/2 c. honey
1/2 c. creamy peanut butter
1/3 c. powdered sugar

Combine apricots, seeds, coconut and cereals in a large bowl; set aside. In a saucepan over medium-high heat, combine butter, honey, peanut butter and powdered sugar. Cook and stir until sugar dissolves. Bring to a boil; simmer for 5 minutes, stirring constantly. Add peanut butter mixture to apricot mixture; mix well. Press mixture into a greased, wax paper-lined 8"x8" baking pan. Refrigerate for several hours. Cut into bars. Makes 16 bars.

Lots of yummy treats begin with peanut butter! If you're looking for an alternative, try sun butter, made from sunflower seeds, or soy nut butter, made from soybeans. Check with your doctor first, to be on the safe side.

Fresh & Delicious Desserts

Ruby's Peanut Butter Cookies

Cassie Hooker
La Porte, TX

We have been making these cookies since I was a little girl. This recipe was handed down to me from my mother when I was married, which is why I call them Ruby's. It's the only peanut butter cookie recipe I have ever used. To me, they are the best!

1 c. shortening
1 c. brown sugar, packed
1 c. sugar
2 eggs, beaten
1 t. vanilla extract

1 c. creamy peanut butter
3 c. all-purpose flour
2 t. baking soda
1/2 t. salt

In a large bowl, thoroughly blend shortening, sugars, eggs and vanilla. Stir in peanut butter. Add remaining ingredients and stir together. Shape dough into one-inch balls; place on baking sheets sprayed with non-stick vegetable spray. Flatten cookies with a floured fork. Bake at 350 degrees for 8 to 10 minutes. Makes about 4 dozen.

Keep cookies tender and moist! Place a slice of bread in the cookie jar or storage bag and your treats will stay soft.

FRESH FARMHOUSE
Recipes

Fresh Peach Bread with Vanilla Glaze

Nichole Sullivan
Santa Fe, TX

One day, my dad & I stopped by a farmers' market and bought a small bucket of fresh Georgia peaches. We were able to take a sample taste while there, and boy howdy! They were not only delicious, they were so juicy that it ran down your hand with each bite! I thought I'd set aside a few to make a sweet quick bread for dessert. This scrumptious recipe is what I came up with...enjoy!

2 c. all-purpose flour
1 t. baking powder
1 t. baking soda
1/2 t. salt
1 t. cinnamon
1/2 c. butter

1-3/4 c. sugar
2 eggs, beaten
1 t. vanilla extract
4 c. peaches, peeled, pitted
 and diced

In a small bowl, sift together flour, baking powder, baking soda, salt and cinnamon; set aside. In a larger bowl, blend together butter and sugar. Add eggs and vanilla; mix well. Slowly add half of flour mixture to butter mixture; stir to combine. Add remaining flour mixture; mix just until well moistened. With a wooden spoon, stir in peaches just until evenly distributed. Divide batter evenly between 2 greased and floured 9"x5" loaf pans. Bake at 325 degrees for one hour, or until a knife tip inserted in center comes out clean. Cool loaves in pans on a wire rack for about 10 minutes; turn out onto rack. Drizzle with Vanilla Glaze. Makes 2 loaves.

Vanilla Glaze:

1/2 c. powdered sugar
1 t. vanilla extract

3 T. milk

Combine all ingredients in a small bowl. Stir until well blended.

Fresh & Delicious Desserts

Apple-Peanut Butter Cookies

Joyceann Dreibelbis
Wooster, OH

These spiced peanut butter cookies are great for any gathering. They're crisp on the outside and soft inside, and so easy to make!

1/2 c. shortening	1-1/2 c. all-purpose flour
1/2 c. crunchy peanut butter	1/2 t. baking soda
1/2 c. sugar	1/2 t. salt
1/2 c. brown sugar, packed	1/2 t. cinnamon
1 egg, beaten	1/2 c. apple, peeled, cored
1/2 t. vanilla extract	and grated

In a large bowl, blend shortening, peanut butter and sugars until light and fluffy. Beat in egg and vanilla. In a separate bowl, combine remaining ingredients except apple; gradually add to shortening mixture and mix well. Stir in apple. Drop dough by rounded tablespoonfuls onto greased baking sheets, 2 inches apart. Bake at 375 degrees for 10 minutes, or until golden. Cool on baking sheets for 5 minutes before removing to wire racks. Makes about 2 dozen.

A big homemade cookie makes a sweet after-dinner treat.
Place in a cellophane bag tied closed with a ribbon and lay
at place settings. Family & friends will feel extra special!

FRESH FARMHOUSE
Recipes

Pecan Tassies

Melissa Currie
Phoenix, AZ

When we lived in Texas where pecans are so plentiful, my sweet mama would make these little bite-size pecan pies every year for Christmas.

1/2 c. butter, softened
   and divided
3-oz. pkg. cream cheese,
   softened
1 c. all-purpose flour

3/4 c. brown sugar, packed
1 egg, beaten
1 T. vanilla extract
1/4 t. salt
2/3 c. pecans, finely chopped

In a bowl, combine 6 tablespoons butter, cream cheese and flour; mix well and form into a ball. Cover and refrigerate for one hour. Form into 24 half-inch balls. Press each ball into the bottom and sides of an ungreased mini muffin cup; set aside. In another bowl, combine brown sugar, egg, remaining butter, vanilla and salt. Mix well with a fork. Add one tablespoon of filling to each mini crust; top with pecans. Bake at 375 degrees for 20 minutes, or until golden. Makes 2 dozen.

Dessert in a dash...spoon ice cream into serving dishes.
Top with fresh berries, toasted almonds and a drizzle
of honey. Garnish with a sprig of mint...yum!

Fresh & Delicious Desserts

Summer Squash Pie

Sandy Mason
Dunn, NC

I take this delicious pie to family gatherings and everyone loves it. I like to serve this to people who don't like squash...I pass it off as a lemon custard. They are really surprised to know that it's made from yellow summer squash, right from my very own garden!

6 to 8 yellow squash, sliced
1/2 c. butter
1 c. sugar
1 T. self-rising flour
1 t. lemon extract

2 eggs, beaten
2 9-inch pie crusts, unbaked
Garnish: whipped topping or
    vanilla ice cream

In a 2-quart saucepan, cover squash with water. Bring to a boil over medium-high heat; simmer until soft. Drain; transfer squash to a blender and process until puréed. Add butter, sugar, flour, extract and eggs to blender; process until well blended. Divide mixture between unbaked pie crusts. Bake at 375 degrees for 60 to 68 minutes, until set and golden. Cool pies on a wire rack for about 15 minutes; cut into wedges. Serve topped with whipped topping or a scoop of ice cream. Serves 8.

A small spice rack is just right for a sweet
collection of pie birds.

Danish Apple Bars

Glenna Ver Steeg
Hancock, MN

These bars are yummy! They were a family favorite at coffee time on the farm when I was growing up, and have been enjoyed by four generations of the Johnson family. My memories of fall were filling the silo, harvesting crops and gathering garden produce.

2-1/2 c. all-purpose flour
1 c. plus 1-1/2 T. sugar, divided
1 t. salt
1 c. butter
1 egg
1/2 c. milk, or as needed

1 to 1-1/2 c. corn flake cereal, crushed
8 baking apples, cored and thinly sliced
1 t. cinnamon
2 egg whites

In a large bowl, mix flour, 1-1/2 tablespoons sugar and salt; cut in butter with a fork and set aside. Beat egg in a measuring cup; add enough milk to equal 1/2 cup. Add egg mixture to flour mixture; stir well. Divide dough into 2 parts. On a floured surface, roll out one dough ball into a 15-inch by 11-inch rectangle. Place in an ungreased 15"x11" jelly-roll pan. Sprinkle crushed cereal over dough; arrange apple slices on top. Combine remaining sugar and cinnamon; sprinkle over apples. Roll out remaining dough; place on top and press edges to seal. In a separate bowl, beat egg whites until foamy; drizzle on top. Bake at 350 degrees for one hour. Cool; cut into bars. Makes 2-1/2 to 3 dozen.

For the best apple desserts, you can always count on
Granny Smith, Fuji, Jonathan, Winesap, Braeburn,
Rome Beauty and Pippin apples.

Fresh & Delicious Desserts

Mixed-Berry Cheesecake

Penny Sherman
Ava, MO

My daughters and I love to go to a nearby farmers' market for juicy fresh-picked berries. This is our favorite way to use them! I like to garnish each slice with a dollop of whipped cream and one perfect strawberry.

9-inch frozen pie crust, unbaked
1 lb. strawberries, hulled
   and divided
1/2 c. blueberries
3/4 c. sugar, divided
1 T. cornstarch
juice of 1 lemon
8-oz. pkg. cream cheese,
   softened
2/3 c. sour cream
1 t. vanilla extract
Optional: whipped cream

Bake pie crust according to package directions; cool completely. Meanwhile, chop half of strawberries; slice remaining strawberries and set aside. In a saucepan, combine chopped strawberries, blueberries, 1/2 cup sugar, cornstarch and lemon juice. Cook over medium heat, stirring constantly, until thickened. Remove from heat. Add sliced strawberries to mixture; stir gently until coated and set aside. In a bowl, combine cream cheese, sour cream, remaining sugar and vanilla. Beat with an electric mixer on medium speed until completely blended and smooth. Spread cream cheese mixture in the bottom of cooled crust; spoon berry mixture over cream cheese mixture. Cover and refrigerate for 2 to 3 hours. Cut into wedges. Garnish with whipped cream, if desired. Makes 6 to 8 servings.

Use a plastic drinking straw to hull strawberries quickly.
Just push the straw through the bottom end and
the leafy green top will pop right off.

FRESH FARMHOUSE
Recipes

Molasses Sugar Cookies

Karen Antonides
Gahanna, OH

My mom always liked cookies with a little bit of spice. She was fond of cinnamon and cloves. Often, our house would smell of spice, especially around the holidays! It was always such a warm, welcoming aroma when coming in from the cold, back on the farm in South Dakota.

3/4 c. shortening
1 c. sugar
1/4 c. molasses
1 egg, beaten
2 c. all-purpose flour
2 t. baking soda

1 t. cinnamon
1/2 t. ground cloves
1/2 t. ground ginger
1/2 t. salt
Garnish: additional sugar

Melt shortening in a small saucepan over low heat; add to a large bowl and cool. Add sugar, molasses and egg; beat well and set aside. In another bowl, sift together flour, baking soda, spices and salt. Add to shortening mixture; mix well. Cover and chill for 3 hours. Form dough into one-inch balls and roll in sugar. Arrange dough balls on greased baking sheets, 2 inches apart. Bake at 375 degrees for 8 to 10 minutes. Cool on wire racks. Makes 3 to 4 dozen.

Baking together is a fun family activity and a great choice for kids just starting to learn how to cook. As you measure and mix, be sure to share any stories about hand-me-down recipes. You'll be creating memories as well as sweet treats!

Fresh & Delicious Desserts

Oatmeal Lemon Crispies

Lisa Barger
Conroe, TX

A delicious old-time recipe out of an old cookbook from years back. It's still my favorite!

1 c. butter, softened
1 c. sugar
1 egg, beaten
1 t. vanilla extract
1 t. lemon extract

1-2/3 c. all-purpose flour
1/4 t. salt
1 c. old-fashioned oats,
    uncooked

In a large bowl, combine butter, sugar, egg and extracts. Beat with an electric mixer on medium speed. Turn mixer to low speed; slowly beat in flour and salt. Stir in oats. Drop dough by tablespoons onto parchment paper-lined baking sheets, 2 inches apart. Bake at 375 degrees for 7 to 10 minutes, until edges are lightly golden. Remove cookies to cool on wire racks. Store in a tightly covered container. Makes 3 dozen.

Sesame Cookies

Irene Robinson
Cincinnati, OH

These tender cookies can be topped with any flavor of fruit preserves. For variety, substitute chopped pecans for sesame seed.

1 c. butter, softened
1/2 c. sugar
1 t. almond extract
2 c. all-purpose flour

1/2 t. salt
1 c. sesame seed
6 T. strawberry preserves

In a bowl, beat butter and sugar until light and fluffy. Stir in extract. Add flour and salt; mix well. Shape dough into balls by rounded tablespoonfuls. Roll in sesame seed; place on ungreased baking sheets. Make an indentation in centers of cookies; spoon a small amount of preserves into centers. Bake at 400 degrees for 10 to 12 minutes, until golden. Makes 3 dozen.

FRESH FARMHOUSE
Recipes

Carrot Cake Whoopie Pies
Mel Chencharick
Julian, PA

My family will eat Whoopie Pies whenever and wherever! One of the things I like about them is that they freeze well. When we were growing up, we used to just go to the freezer, pull out a frozen Whoopie Pie and eat it...yummy!

1-1/2 c. all-purpose flour	1 egg, beaten
1 t. baking powder	1/2 c. light brown sugar, packed
1/2 t. baking soda	1 t. vanilla extract
2 t. cinnamon	1-1/2 c. carrots, peeled and
1/4 c. butter, softened	grated
2 T. canola oil	1/2 c. raisins

In a bowl, whisk together flour, baking powder, baking soda and cinnamon; set aside. In a large bowl, blend together butter, oil, egg, brown sugar and vanilla. Fold in carrots and raisins. Add flour mixture to butter mixture; stir until combined. Lightly coat 2 large baking sheets with shortening; lightly dust with flour or line with parchment paper. Spoon batter into 24 mounds onto baking sheets, flattening slightly. Bake at 350 degrees for 10 to 12 minutes, until lightly golden and tops spring back when lightly touched. Remove cookies to wire racks; cool for at least 5 minutes. Sandwich cookies together in pairs with Frosting. Makes one dozen.

Frosting:

8-oz. pkg. cream cheese, softened	1/4 c. powdered sugar
	1 t. vanilla extract

Combine all ingredients; beat until smooth.

Plump up raisins for extra moist, tender cookies. Soak them in warm water for 3 to 5 minutes, drain and add to recipe.

Fresh & Delicious Desserts

Rhubarb Cheesecake Bars

*Hannah Thiry
Luxemburg, WI*

A luscious way to use some of that rhubarb from your garden! It's very easy to make.

2 c. all-purpose flour
1 c. old-fashioned oats,
   uncooked
1 c. brown sugar, packed
1/2 t. cinnamon, divided
1/2 c. butter

2 8-oz. pkgs. cream cheese,
   softened
2 c. sugar
2 eggs, beaten
2 c. rhubarb, diced

In a large bowl, mix flour, oats, brown sugar and 1/4 teaspoon cinnamon. Use a fork to cut in butter until coarse and crumbly. Press 2/3 of crumb mixture into the bottom of an ungreased 13"x9" baking pan; set aside. In another large bowl, beat together cream cheese, sugar and eggs until smooth. Add remaining cinnamon; gently fold in rhubarb. Spoon rhubarb mixture over crust; sprinkle with remaining crumb mixture. Bake at 350 degrees for 45 minutes, or until a knife tip inserted in the center comes out clean. Cool; cut into bars. Makes one dozen.

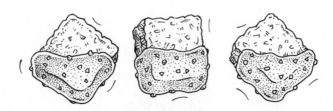

Dress up bar cookies with a yummy glaze. Combine
1/2 cup white chocolate chips and one teaspoon shortening
in a microwave-safe bowl. Microwave on high for
one minute, stir, then drizzle over bars.

FRESH FARMHOUSE
Recipes

Hilda's Zucchini Brownies

Emilie Britton
New Bremen, OH

I received this recipe from a dear friend. We meet with a group of other women to make and donate fleece blankets. Food is the topic of discussion at many of our meet-ups, and Hilda shared this delicious recipe with me.

4 eggs, beaten
1-1/4 c. oil
2 c. sugar
2 c. all-purpose flour
2 t. baking soda

1 t. salt
2 T. baking cocoa
1 t. vanilla extract
3 c. zucchini, grated
1 c. chopped nuts

In a large bowl, mix together all ingredients. Spread in a greased 17"x11" jelly-roll pan. Bake at 350 degrees for 25 to 30 minutes. Set pan on a wire rack; cool completely. Spread Topping over cooled brownies; cut into squares. Makes 3 to 4 dozen.

Topping:

3-oz. pkg. cream cheese,
    softened
1/2 c. butter, softened

2 c. powdered sugar
2 T. baking cocoa

Beat together all ingredients until smooth.

In brownie recipes, try using applesauce in place of oil.
It makes brownies extra moist, with fewer calories,
and works just as well as oil.

Fresh & Delicious Desserts

Pecan Pie Cookies

Tracee Cummins
Georgetown, TX

These cookies are a family favorite. A great combination of pie and cookie, from the buttery crust to the rich pecan filling...they can't be beat!

2 c. all-purpose flour
1/2 c. powdered sugar
1 c. chilled butter, cut into
   1-inch slices
14-oz. can sweetened condensed
   milk

1 egg, beaten
1 t. vanilla extract
8-oz. pkg. almond brickle
   baking chips
1 c. chopped pecans

Combine flour and powdered sugar in a food processor; add butter and pulse until a crumbly dough forms. Press dough firmly into the bottom of a greased 13"x9" glass baking pan. Bake at 325 degrees for 15 minutes. Meanwhile, in a large bowl, beat condensed milk, egg and vanilla until well blended. Stir in chips and pecans; spread mixture evenly over hot crust. Bake at 325 degrees for 25 minutes, or until golden. Cool in pan on a wire rack; cut into bars. Makes 1-1/2 dozen.

Stock up on ice cream flavors, nuts and toppings... spend an afternoon making banana splits and memories with the kids!

Tracey's Pear Cake

Tracey Gasaway
Trion, GA

This is a yummy recipe I used when the two pear trees
in our yard were producing more pears than I knew what
to do with. This cake freezes really well.

1 c. sugar
1 c. brown sugar, packed
3 eggs, beaten
1 c. oil
2 t. vanilla extract
3 c. all-purpose flour

1 t. salt
1 t. baking soda
2 t. cinnamon
4 c. pears, peeled, cored
   and sliced

In a large bowl, mix all ingredients by hand in order given. Pour batter
into a greased 13"x9" baking pan. Bake at 350 degrees for 45 minutes.
Pour Topping over cake; return to oven for 4 minutes. Cut into squares.
Makes 15 servings.

Topping:

1/2 c. butter
1/2 c. brown sugar, packed

1/4 c. milk

Combine all ingredients in a saucepan. Bring to a low boil for 3 minutes,
stirring until brown sugar dissolves.

Core apples and pears in a jiffy...cut the fruit in half,
then use a melon baller to scoop out the center.

Fresh & Delicious Desserts

Spiced Country Plum Pie

Sharon Demers
Bruce Crossing, MI

This pie is delicious! Coriander gives it a unique and pleasant flavor.

2 9-inch pie crusts, unbaked
4 c. Italian prune plums, halved
   and pitted
2 t. lemon juice
1/2 c. sugar

2 t. quick-cooking tapioca,
   uncooked
1/2 t. cinnamon
1/2 t. ground coriander
2 t. butter, melted

Roll out one crust and fit into a 9" pie plate; do not trim edges. Set aside. In a large bowl, combine plums and lemon juice; toss to coat and set aside. In a small bowl, combine sugar, tapioca and spices. Add sugar mixture to plums; toss to mix and let stand for 15 minutes. Spoon plum mixture into pie crust, mounding slightly in the center. Drizzle with melted butter. Roll out remaining crust and place on top of pie; pinch edges to seal. Trim and flute edges; make several slits with a knife tip. Bake at 425 degrees for 15 minutes. Reduce heat to 375 degrees; continue baking for 35 minutes, or until pastry is golden. Let cool on a wire rack; cut into wedges. Makes 8 to 10 servings.

An intricate lattice pie crust is glorious, but there's an easier way. Simply lay half the lattice strips across the pie filling in one direction, then lay the remaining strips at right angles. No weaving required!

FRESH FARMHOUSE
Recipes

Lemon Chess Pie

*Delores Lakes
Mansfield, OH*

I love this pie served with fresh red fruit or fruit sauce...strawberries, red raspberries, pomegranates, just beautiful!

2 c. sugar
1 T. all-purpose flour
1 T. cornmeal
4 eggs, beaten
1/4 c. butter, melted

1/4 c. milk
1/4 c. lemon juice
zest of 1-1/2 lemons
9-inch pie crust, unbaked

In a large bowl, toss sugar, flour and cornmeal with a fork. Add remaining ingredients except pie crust; mix well. Pour into crust. Bake at 450 degrees for 10 minutes. Reduce heat to 350 degrees; bake another 30 minutes. Serve at room temperature or slightly chilled. Cut into wedges. Serves 8.

Fresh Strawberry Marmalade Sauce

*Hope Davenport
Portland, TX*

This scrumptious sauce is a great topping for vanilla ice cream, cheesecake, waffles or crepes. You might want to double the recipe!

2 pts. strawberries, hulled
    and quartered
2 T. sugar

1/2 c. orange marmalade
1 T. lemon juice
2 t. balsamic vinegar

In a large bowl, stir together strawberries and sugar; let stand for about 5 minutes. Stir in marmalade, lemon juice and vinegar. Cover and chill for one hour. Makes about 3 cups.

A sugar shaker is handy for dusting fresh-baked desserts with powdered sugar.

Fresh &
Delicious Desserts

Lemon & Basil Cookies

Lisa Ashton
Aston, PA

I wanted to use up some of the basil I have growing in my garden. These turned out to have an interesting taste...I'll make them again!

1 c. fresh basil, finely chopped
2 c. sugar, divided
1 c. butter

1/4 c. lemon juice
1 egg, beaten
6 c. all-purpose flour

In a bowl, combine basil and 1/4 cup sugar; set aside. In a large bowl, beat butter with an electric mixer on medium speed until creamy. Add 1-1/2 cups sugar; beat until well blended. Add lemon juice and egg; mix until well blended. Gradually add flour and basil mixture; mix well. Shape dough into one-inch balls; roll in remaining sugar. Place on parchment paper-lined baking sheets, about 2 inches apart. Bake at 350 degrees for about 8 to 10 minutes. Remove to wire racks to cool. Makes 6 dozen.

Rosemary Shortbread

Evelyn DeLutis
Bridgewater, MA

This is so easy to make, and delicious with a cup of hot tea. All ingredients go into a food processor. Because the recipe is so quick, I usually double it and freeze half. Don't care for rosemary? Use orange or lemon zest instead.

1/3 c. sugar
1 c. all-purpose flour
2 T. fresh rosemary, chopped

1/2 c. chilled butter, cut
into chunks

Add all ingredients to a food processor. Process briefly, just until combined; mixture will be crumbly. Press dough firmly into a lightly greased 9" pie plate. Score top into 8 wedges; do not cut through. Bake at 325 degrees for 30 minutes, or until edges are golden, starting to check for doneness at 25 minutes. Cool for 5 minutes; cut into wedges. Makes 8 servings.

FRESH FARMHOUSE
Recipes

Buttery Triple-Berry Cobbler   *Lori Roggenbuck*
Ubly, MI

I originally made this recipe for family members who were coming all the way from Tennessee to visit. It's been a huge hit, served up warm with a dollop of vanilla ice cream.

1/3 c. butter
1-1/2 c. all-purpose flour
1-1/2 c. sugar
1-1/2 c. milk
2 t. baking powder
1/2 t. cinnamon
1/2 t. salt

5 c. fresh blueberries,
  strawberries and raspberries,
  chopped
1/3 c. brown sugar, packed
Optional: 1/3 c. chopped pecans
Garnish: vanilla ice cream or
  whipped cream

Add butter to a 13"x9" baking pan. Place in oven set to 375 degrees to melt while preheating. Meanwhile, in a large bowl, combine flour, sugar, milk, baking powder, cinnamon and salt. Whisk together until a thin, smooth batter forms. Pour batter into baking pan over melted butter; do not stir. Butter will rise up around the surface of the batter. Sprinkle berries evenly over batter; sprinkle with brown sugar and pecans, if using. Bake at 375 degrees for 45 to 60 minutes, until golden and a toothpick inserted in the center tests done. Serve warm, garnished as desired. Serves 8 to 10.

Try all the different kinds of local berries you may find at local farmstands. Mulberries, huckleberries, boysenberries, lingonberries, loganberries, dewberries, cloudberries... they're all delightful!

208

Fresh & Delicious Desserts

Gilda's Strawberry Dessert

Mary Lynn Rabon
Mobile, AL

This is a light and delicious dessert. My grandmother made a dessert that was something like this for many occasions. My cousin Gilda tweaked it and it has become very popular with my own family.

6-oz. pkg. strawberry gelatin mix
2 c. boiling water
2 c. cold water
1-1/2 qts. strawberries, hulled
    and sliced
sugar to taste

1-1/2 bakery angel food cakes or
    pound cakes, torn into large
    pieces and divided
16-oz. container frozen whipped
    topping, divided

Place gelatin mix in a large bowl. Add boiling water and stir for 2 minutes, or until completely dissolved. Stir in cold water; cover and refrigerate until partially set. Meanwhile, in another bowl, sweeten strawberries with sugar to taste; cover and refrigerate. To assemble, add half of cake pieces to a large clear glass bowl. Spoon half of strawberries over cake; pour half of partially set gelatin on top and spread with half of whipped topping. Repeat layering, ending with whipped topping. Cover and refrigerate for one hour or more. Makes 10 to 12 servings.

Host a dessert party for family & friends on a sunny afternoon. Set tables under shady trees and layer them with quilts or checked tablecloths. Have everyone bring their favorite dessert...sure to be fun for all!

FRESH FARMHOUSE
Recipes

Vanilla-Cinnamon Sauce Fruit Cup

Janis Parr
Ontario, Canada

This dessert is delicious, good for you, and simple to make...
I promise! Strawberries, raspberries, peaches, pears,
bananas and mangoes are all delicious in this recipe.

1/2 c. sugar
2 T. cornstarch
4-inch cinnamon stick
12-oz. can evaporated milk

1-1/2 t. vanilla extract
6 c. assorted soft fresh fruit,
   sliced or cubed

In a saucepan, combine sugar, cornstarch and cinnamon stick in a saucepan. Gradually stir in evaporated milk. Cook over medium heat, stirring constantly, until mixture comes just to a boil and thickens slightly. Remove from heat; remove cinnamon stick and stir in vanilla. Allow to cool; cover and refrigerate for 2 hours. To serve, arrange fruit in dessert dishes; top with cooled sauce. Refrigerate any leftover sauce in a covered container for up to 4 days. Serves 6.

Serve up puddings and parfaits in mini Mason jars.
Garnish with whipped topping and a sprig of fresh mint...
fun for picnics and potlucks!

Fresh &
Delicious Desserts

Mom's Stewed Rhubarb

Dawna Greenham
Ontario, Canada

One of my fondest childhood memories is of going to my mom's backyard garden and picking fresh rhubarb from the big patch she had growing there. There was nothing better than fresh rhubarb, dipped in sugar, clutched tightly in my small hand as I happily enjoyed my fresh-from-the-garden treat. That is, until, Mom made stewed rhubarb and served it over vanilla ice cream...my entire view changed!

4 c. rhubarb, chopped   1 c. water
1/2 c. sugar

Combine all ingredients in a saucepan. Simmer over medium-high heat, stirring occasionally, until rhubarb is cooked down into a velvety sauce. Serve warm or chilled over ice cream, mixed into hot oatmeal or used as a filling for tarts. Makes 4 servings.

Granny's Raspberry Pie

Judy Lange
Imperial, PA

*Going to Granny's house after church, I could hardly wait
to dig into her delicious pie!*

35 large marshmallows   12-oz. container frozen whipped
1/2 c. milk   topping, thawed
10-oz. pkg. fresh raspberries   9-inch graham cracker crust

In a large microwave-safe bowl, combine marshmallows and milk. Microwave on high for one to 2 minutes; stir until smooth. Fold in raspberries; fold in whipped topping. Spoon mixture into crust. Cover and refrigerate for 4 hours or overnight. Cut into wedges. Makes 8 servings.

Short and sweet...top sliced ripe peaches with a drizzle of honey and a sprinkling of cinnamon. Yum!

211

FRESH FARMHOUSE
Recipes

Chocolate Velvet Pie

Tina Wright
Atlanta, GA

*This pie is irresistible! My Aunt Betty always brought it
to family gatherings...we loved it.*

9-inch frozen pie crust, unbaked
2 1-oz. sqs. unsweetened
  baking chocolate
14-oz. can sweetened condensed
  milk

2 eggs, well beaten
1 c. water
2 t. vanilla extract
Garnish: whipped cream
Optional: chocolate curls

Bake pie crust according to package directions; set aside. Meanwhile, in
a heavy saucepan over medium heat, melt chocolate with condensed
milk; stir well and remove from heat. Stir in eggs; stir in water and
vanilla. Pour into warm crust. Bake at 400 degrees for 10 minutes.
Reduce oven temperature to 300 degrees; bake another 20 minutes, or
until center is set. Cool; cover and chill thoroughly. Cut into wedges.
Garnish with a dollop of whipped cream and chocolate curls, if desired.
Makes 8 servings.

Homemade ice cream sandwiches! Spread softened ice cream
on one cookie and top with another cookie. Roll the edges in
candy sprinkles, wrap in plastic wrap and freeze until solid.

Fresh & Delicious Desserts

Brown Sugar Drops

Jennifer Bower
Winston-Salem, NC

These cookies are delicious! My grandmother, Levie Shelton, had hundreds of recipes pasted into notebooks that she'd clipped from magazines and newspapers. But her best recipes were the ones that she had handwritten on scraps of paper...the ones that were made often and enjoyed by many. This is one of those recipes. So glad I could share it with you!

1 egg, well beaten	1/4 t. baking soda
1 c. brown sugar, packed	1/4 t. salt
1 t. vanilla extract	1-1/2 c. English walnuts,
1/2 c. all-purpose flour	chopped

In a large bowl, stir together egg, brown sugar and vanilla. Add flour, baking soda and salt; mix thoroughly. Add walnuts and stir again until evenly mixed. Drop dough by teaspoonfuls onto greased and floured baking sheets. Bake at 350 degrees for 7 to 9 minutes, just until starting to turn golden at the edges. Watch closely after 5 minutes. Remove cookies to wire racks for cooling. Makes about 4 dozen.

You're never too old for a tea party! Make iced cookies and sugar-dusted tea cakes...fill dainty teacups with hot spice tea. What a delightful way to spend time with your sisters, cousins and girlfriends of all ages...and don't forget Mom and Grandma!

FRESH FARMHOUSE
Recipes

Apple Pudding with Brown Sugar Sauce

Gerri Roth
Flushing, MI

This is a scrumptious old recipe my mother used to make when I was a child. I still love to make it in the fall with fresh-picked apples. For an extra-thick dessert, I often double the recipe and bake it in the same size pan.

2 eggs
1-1/2 c. sugar
1 t. vanilla extract
1-1/2 c. all-purpose flour

2 t. baking powder
1/8 t. salt
2 c. apples, cored and chopped

In a large bowl, beat eggs lightly. Add sugar and vanilla; stir well and set aside. In another bowl, combine flour, baking powder and salt; mix well. Add flour mixture to egg mixture and stir well. Mixture will be very stiff. Fold in apples; mixture will become thinner. Spread batter in a greased 8"x8" baking pan. Bake at 375 degrees for 35 to 40 minutes. Serve warm or at room temperature, topped with warm Brown Sugar Sauce. Makes 9 servings.

Brown Sugar Sauce:

1 c. brown sugar, packed
2 T. all-purpose flour
1 c. water

2 T. butter, diced
1 t. vanilla extract

Combine brown sugar and flour in a microwave-safe bowl; whisk in water. Microwave on high for 4 minutes, whisking after every minute, or until thickened. Stir in butter and vanilla.

Come and share a pot of tea,
my home is warm
and my friendship's free.
—Emilie Barnes

Fresh & Delicious Desserts

Lazy-Day Raspberry Cobbler

Judith Smith
Bellevue, WA

I received this easy recipe at a social gathering in the early 1980s. Since then, I have made it many times for family gatherings.

1/2 c. butter, melted	1/4 salt
1-1/2 c. sugar, divided	3/4 c. milk
1 c. all-purpose flour	3 c. fresh raspberries
1-1/2 t. baking powder	Garnish: vanilla ice cream

Spread melted butter in a 2-quart deep-dish casserole dish; set aside. In a bowl, mix together one cup sugar, flour, baking powder, salt and milk; stir well. Pour batter over melted butter, but do not stir. Pour raspberries over batter, again do not stir. Sprinkle remaining sugar over all; do not stir. Bake at 350 degrees for 40 to 45 minutes, until golden and batter has risen to the top. Serve warm, topped with ice cream. Makes 8 to 10 servings.

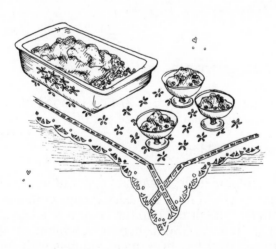

For flavor and texture when baking desserts, butter is better! If you prefer to use margarine, though, be sure to use regular stick margarine rather than reduced-fat margarine, which has a higher water content.

FRESH FARMHOUSE
Recipes

Beth's Fresh Orange Cake

Karen Dennis
Mount Vernon, OH

*This cake is so good! We took an old family recipe and tweaked it
a bit with ingredients we had on hand. Delicious!*

3 c. all-purpose flour
3 eggs, beaten
1-1/2 t. vanilla extract
1 t. baking powder
1 c. sugar

1/2 c. butter, melted
zest of 1 orange
2 c. powdered sugar
1 to 2 T. milk

In a large bowl, beat together all ingredients except powdered sugar and
milk. Spread batter in a greased Bundt® pan. Bake at 350 degrees for
30 to 40 minutes, until cake tests done with a toothpick. Let cool.
Combine powdered sugar and milk; mix to a glaze consistency and
drizzle over cake. Cut into slices. Makes 10 to 12 servings.

Caramel Streusel Bars

Vickie
Gooseberry Patch

Ooey-gooey goodness, and easy to make!

2 c. all-purpose flour
3/4 c. light brown sugar, packed
1 egg, beaten
3/4 c. chilled butter, divided

3/4 c. chopped nuts
24 caramels, unwrapped
14-oz. can sweetened condensed
milk

In a large bowl, combine flour, sugar and egg. Cut in 1/2 cup butter with
a fork until crumbly; stir in nuts. Set aside 2 cups crumb mixture; press
remaining crumb mixture firmly into the bottom of a lightly greased
13"x9" baking pan. Bake at 350 degrees for 15 minutes. Meanwhile,
in a heavy saucepan over low heat, melt caramels with condensed
milk and remaining butter. Stir mixture until smooth; pour over crumb
crust. Sprinkle with reserved crumb mixture. Bake at 350 degrees
for 30 minutes, or until bubbly. Cool completely; cut into bars.
Makes 2 to 3 dozen.

Fresh & Delicious Desserts

My Oatmeal Cookies

Ramona Wysong
Barlow, KY

Whether they're plain or filled with raisins, cranberries or butterscotch chips, these cookies are scrumptious.

3/4 c. butter, softened
1 c. light brown sugar, packed
1/2 c. sugar
1 egg
1/4 c. water
1 c. all-purpose flour
1 t. salt
1/2 t. baking soda
1 t. vanilla extract
3 c. quick-cooking oats, uncooked
Optional: 3/4 c. dried cranberries, raisins or butterscotch chips

In a large bowl, blend together butter, sugars and egg. Add water alternately with flour, salt and baking soda; mix well. Stir in vanilla. Stir in oats, blending well. Fold in optional ingredients, if desired. Drop batter by heaping spoonfuls (not a regular measuring teaspoon) onto greased baking sheets. Bake at 350 degrees for 12 to 15 minutes. Makes about 3 dozen.

Keep crisp cookies crisp and soft cookies chewy in a cookie tin...separate the layers with sheets of wax paper.

INDEX

INDEX

INDEX

Find Gooseberry Patch
wherever you are!

www.gooseberrypatch.com

Call us toll-free at 1·800·854·6673

sunny days   fresh-cut grass

floppy straw hats

strawberry picking

twinkling fireflies

smiling sunflowers

county fairs   sun-ripened tomatoes

U.S. to Metric Recipe Equivalents

Volume Measurements

1/4 teaspoon	1 mL
1/2 teaspoon	2 mL
1 teaspoon	5 mL
1 tablespoon = 3 teaspoons	15 mL
2 tablespoons = 1 fluid ounce	30 mL
1/4 cup	60 mL
1/3 cup	75 mL
1/2 cup = 4 fluid ounces	125 mL
1 cup = 8 fluid ounces	250 mL
2 cups = 1 pint =16 fluid ounces	500 mL
4 cups = 1 quart	1 L

Weights

1 ounce	30 g
4 ounces	120 g
8 ounces	225 g
16 ounces = 1 pound	450 g

Oven Temperatures

300° F	150° C
325° F	160° C
350° F	180° C
375° F	190° C
400° F	200° C
450° F	230° C

Baking Pan Sizes

Square

8x8x2 inches	2 L = 20x20x5 cm
9x9x2 inches	2.5 L = 23x23x5 cm

Rectangular

13x9x2 inches	3.5 L = 33x23x5 cm

Loaf

9x5x3 inches	2 L = 23x13x7 cm

Round

8x1-1/2 inches	1.2 L = 20x4 cm
9x1-1/2 inches	1.5 L = 23x4 cm